SCOTS-IRISH LINKS
1575–1725

PART SIX

by
David Dobson

CLEARFIELD

Printed for
Clearfield Company by
Genealogical Publishing Co.
Baltimore, Maryland
2007

ISBN-13: 978-0-8063-5351-7
ISBN-10: 0-8063-5351-1

Made in the United States of America

INTRODUCTION

The Plantation of Ulster by Scots in the seventeenth century is a well-established fact. Genealogists, however, require very specific reference material which is generally missing from the published accounts of the migration of up to 100,000 Scottish Lowlanders to northern Ireland at that time.

Part Six of *Scots-Irish Links, 1575-1725* attempts to identify some of these Scots settlers and is based mainly on contemporary primary source material found in Scotland and Ireland, especially tax records and muster rolls.

Within a few generations, the descendants of these Ulster Scots emigrated in substantial numbers across the Atlantic where, as the Scotch-Irish, they made a major contribution to the settlement and development of Colonial America.

David Dobson
St Andrews, Scotland, 2007.

SOME SHIPPING LINKS

JANET OF GLASGOW, master Walter Cameron, voyaging between Glasgow and Belfast in 1686. [NAS.AC7.7]

KATHERINE OF GLASGOW, master John Wyllie, voyaging between Glasgow to Belfast in 1690. [RPCS.XV.88]

SAMPLE DOCUMENT

Indenture between Sir Hugh Montgomerie of Newton, in the county of Down, knight, on the one part, and George Cunningham of Bally Loherstowe, and Patrick Shaw of Bally Walter, on the other part, by which Sir Hugh conveys to them, on behalf of his 'well-beloved wife', Lady Elizabeth Montgomerie, 'for her better livelihood, maintenance and jointure,' the manor house of Gray Abbey, and all its demesne lands, presently in the occupation of Thomas Agnewe, James McClelland of Auchenhay, Gilbert McClelland or Thomas McClelland, with the whole circuit and precinct of the same in the said county of Down, bounded on the west by the lands of John Cassen, on the north by the great common moss or moor, on the east and south-east by John Peacock's lands, the lands of Black Abbey and Cuthbert Cunninghame's lands, and on the south and south-west by the 'lough' and sea called 'Loughroine', and by Colonel David Boid's lands; also the sum of £200 sterling 'current old money in England' from Sir Hugh's lands in the Great Ards with other provisions.
Dated 28th August 1610.
Signed 'George Cunynghame' 'mother brother to the said lady of the house of Glengarnock'; 'Patrick Schaw', 'her brother-german of the hous of Grinok'.
[Source: Laing Manuscript #1582, Edinburgh University]

SCOTS IRISH LINKS

REFERENCES

ARCHIVES

NA   =   National Archives, London
NAS   =   National Archives of Scotland, Edinburgh
NLS   =   National Library of Scotland, Edinburgh
PCC   =   Prerogative Court of Canterbury

PUBLICATIONS

AG   =   Archaelogical and Historical Collections,
             Ayrshire and Galloway, [Edinburgh, 1895]
CDG   =   Charters and Documents relating to Glasgow,
             [Glasgow, 1906]
CSA   =   Commonwealth State Accounts, Ireland, series
CSPIre   Calendar of State Papers, Ireland, series
DP   =   Doneraile Papers, Cork
DS   =   Scottish Covenanters and Irish Confederates,
             David Stevenson, [Belfast, 1981]
F   =   Fastii Ecclesiae Scoticanae, J. Scott, [Edinburgh,
             1915]
HH   =   Family Papers of the Hunters of Hunterston
HTR   =   Hearth Tax Roll
Laing=   Calendar of the Laing Charters 854-1837,
             [Edinburgh, 1899]
LI   The Lochiel Inventory, 1472-1744, [Edinburgh,
             2000]
PBK   The Presbytery Book of Kirkcaldy, 1630-1653
REA   =   Register of Edinburgh Apprentices
RGS   =   Register of the Great Seal of Scotland, series
RPCS=   Register of the Privy Council of Scotland, series
SBR   =   Extracts of the Records of the Burgh of Stirling,
             [Glasgow, 1887]

SCOTS-IRISH LINKS,

1575-1725

[Part Six]

ADAIR, ALEXANDER, Captain of the Earl of Lindsay's Regiment at Carrickfergus in September 1642. [DS#334]

ADAIR, HELEN, widow of William Adair of Ballymanaoch or Kinhilt, and Archibald Edmonstone of Braidisland, marriage contract dated 17 April 1666. [NAS.GD97.Sec.1/501]

ADAIR, PATRICK, 1624-1695, a Presbyterian minister in Belfast. [NLS.Wod.Fol.XXVI.52]

ADAIR, ROBERT, to swear in constables for the parish of St Connon, 5 July 1631. [NAS.GD97.Sec.1/409]

ADAM, MATTHEW, in the parish of Raphoe, County Donegal, 1665. [HTR]

ADAM, PATRICK, mustered unarmed in the barony of Raphoe, County Donegal, 1630. [Donegal Muster Roll]

ADAM, ROBERT, mustered with a sword in the barony of Raphoe, County Donegal, 1630. [Donegal Muster Roll]

ADAMS, JOHN, master of the Friendship of Belfast from Port Glasgow to Belfast in September 1710. [EUL.Laing.490.120.1]

ADAMS, WILLIAM, a tenant, 1663. [NAS.RH15.91.38C]

ADAMSON, GILBERT, in the barony of Magherasterhana and Clankeilly, County Fermanagh, 1631. [Fermanagh Muster Roll]

ADAMSON, JOHN, 1627. [NAS.RH15.91.39]

ADARE, ROBERT, son and heir of the late William Adare of Ballymanagh, County Antrim, 1661. [CSP.Ire.30.12.1661]

AGNEW, ALEXANDER, son of Alexander Agnew a resident of Ireland, was apprenticed to Robert Selkirk a merchant in Edinburgh on 27 August 1679. [REA]

AGNEW, Sir ANDREW, a landowner in the parish of Kilwaghter, 1652. [NAS.GD154.514]

AGNEW, KATHERINE, a tenant, May 1672. [NAS.RH15.91.40]

AGNEW, PATRICK, in the parish of Kilwaghter, 1652. [NAS.GD154.514]

AGNEW, THOMAS, in Gray Abbey, County Down, 1610. [Laing#1582]

AGNEW, THOMAS, in Belfast, 1686. [NAS.GD154.935]

AICKEN, ROBERT, mustered with a sword and a pike in the barony of Raphoe, County Donegal, 1630. [Donegal Muster Roll]

AIKEN, DAVID, in Dungiven, County Londonderry, 1630. [Dungiven Muster Roll]

AIKEN, WILLIAM, in Anlow, County Londonderry, 9 August 1666. [NAS.RH15.91.40]

AIKENHEAD, JOHN, mustered in the barony of Raphoe, County Donegal, 1630. [Donegal Muster Roll]

AITKEN, WILLIAM, mustered with a sword in the barony of Raphoe, County Donegal, 1630. [Donegal Muster Roll]

ALEXANDER, ANDREW, mariner of the Broswell of Newport, Ireland, 1721. [NAS.AC8.260]

ALEXANDER, JOHN, mustered with sword and pike in the barony of Raphoe, County Donegal, 1630. [Donegal Muster Roll]

ALEXANDER, JOHN, in the parish of Raphoe, County Donegal, 1665. [HTR]

ALEXANDER, JOHN, a tenant on William Conyngham's lands in County Londonderry, 1683. [DP/Lenox-Conyngham pp]

ALEXANDER, RICHARD, son of James Alexander from Glasgow, was baptised on 20 March 1667 in Blaris, Lisburn, County Down. [Blaris Parish Register]

ALEXANDER, WILLIAM, in the parish of Raphoe, County Donegal, 1665. [HTR]

ALLAN, ALEXANDER, mustered with a sword in the barony of Raphoe, County Donegal, 1630. [Donegal Muster Roll]

ALLAN, HUGH, mustered unarmed in the barony of Raphoe, County Donegal, 1630. [Donegal Muster Roll]

ALLAN, JOHN, leased part of Gray Abbey lands known as Ballibrier and Ballimainstra from William Edmonstone of Braidisland, 16 October 1623. [NAS.GD97/Sec.1/378]

ALLAN, JOHN, mustered with a sword in the barony of Raphoe, County Donegal, 1630. [Donegal Muster Roll]

ALLAN, JOHN, of Kiltoell, in the parish of Raphoe, County Donegal, 1665. [HTR]

ALLAN, ROBERT, a merchant in Belfast, 1726. [NAS.AC9.967]

ALLASON, ANDREW, in the parish of Raphoe, County Donegal, 1665. [HTR]

ALLASON, JOHN, mustered with sword and pike in the barony of Raphoe, County Donegal, 1630. [Donegal Muster Roll]

ALLASON, JOHN, mustered unarmed in the barony of Raphoe, County Donegal, 1630. [Donegal Muster Roll]

ALLASON, THOMAS, mustered with sword and pike in the barony of Raphoe, County Donegal, 1630. [Donegal Muster Roll]

ALLASON, ..., heirs, from Windyedge, parish of Avondale, probably a Covenanting refugee, to Ireland by 1683. [RPCS.VIII.653]

ALLEN, JAMES, mustered with a sword and snaphance in the barony of Raphoe, County Donegal, 1630. [Donegal Muster Roll]

ALLEN, JOHN, mustered with a sword in the barony of Raphoe, County Donegal, 1630. [Donegal Muster Roll]

ALLYSON, GEORGE, mustered unarmed in the barony of Raphoe, County Donegal, 1630. [Donegal Muster Roll]

ALLYSON, JOHN, mustered in the barony of Raphoe, County Donegal, 1630. [Donegal Muster Roll]

ANDERSON, ALEXANDER, in the barony of Magheraboy, County Fermanagh, 1631. [Fermanagh Muster Roll]

ANDERSON, ANDREW, a tenant on William Conyngham's lands in County Londonderry, 1683. [DP/Lenox-Conyngham pp]

ANDERSON, JOHN, of Drumiel, leased lands in Glencorme from Archibald Edmonstone of Braidisland, 15 July 1627. [NAS.GD97.Sec.1/388]

4

ANDERSON, JOHN, a tenant on William Conyngham's lands in County Londonderry, 1683. [DP/Lenox-Conyngham pp]

ANDERSON, JOHN, a carpenter in Strabane, County Tyrone, in March 1688. [NAS.AC7.9]

ANDERSON, ROBERT, absent from Hamilton, probably a Covenanting refugee, to Ireland by 1683. [RPCS.VIII.651]

ANDERSON, THOMAS, in the barony of Magheraboy, County Fermanagh, 1631. [Fermanagh Muster Roll]

ANDERSON, THOMAS, in Anlow, County Londonderry, 9 August 1666. [NAS.RH15.91.40]

ANDREW, JOHN, in the parish of Kilwaghter, 1652. [NAS.GD154.514]

ARBUCKLE, JAMES, a merchant in Belfast, 1722. [NAS.AC9.849]

ARCHIBALD, JAMES, in the parish of Kilwaghter, 1652. [NAS.GD154.514]

ARCKLY, JOHN, mustered with sword in the barony of Raphoe, County Donegal, 1630. [Donegal Muster Roll]

ARCLES, JOHN, the elder of Cloghroy, in the parish of Raphoe, County Donegal, 1665. [HTR]

ARCLES, JOHN, the younger, in the parish of Raphoe, County Donegal, 1665. [HTR]

ARMOR, THOMAS, mustered with a sword in the barony of Raphoe, County Donegal, 1630. [Donegal Muster Roll]

ARMSTRONG, ADAM, in the barony of Magherasterhana and Clankeilly, County Fermanagh, 1631. [Fermanagh Muster Roll]

ARMSTRONG, ALEXANDER, in the barony of
Magheraboy, County Fermanagh, 1631. [Fermanagh
Muster Roll]

ARMSTRONG, ARCHIBALD, in the barony of
Magheraboy, County Fermanagh, 1631. [Fermanagh
Muster Roll]

ARMSTRONG, CHARLES, of Mount Armstrong, Ireland,
1722. [LI#406]

ARMSTRONG, GEORGE, in the barony of Magheraboy,
County Fermanagh, 1631. [Fermanagh Muster Roll]

ARMSTRONG, JAMES, in the barony of Magherasterhana
and Clankeilly, County Fermanagh, 1631. [Fermanagh
Muster Roll]

ARMSTRONG, JAMES, in the barony of Magheraboy,
County Fermanagh, 1631. [Fermanagh Muster Roll]

ARMSTRONG, JOHN, in the barony of Magheraboy, County
Fermanagh, 1631. [Fermanagh Muster Roll]

ARMSTRONG, LANCELOT, in the barony of Magheraboy,
County Fermanagh, 1631. [Fermanagh Muster Roll]

ARMSTRONG, ROBERT, in the barony of Magherasterhana
and Clankeilly, County Fermanagh, 1631. [Fermanagh
Muster Roll]

ARMSTRONG, THOMAS, born 1647, son of George
Armstrong, died 28 May 1675. [Clogher Cathedral
gravestone]

ARMSTRONG, Sir THOMAS, in Dublin, probate 1676 PCC

ARMSTRONG, the widow, a tenant, May 1672.
[NAS.RH15.91.40]

ARNOT, ANDREW, mustered with sword in the barony of
Raphoe, County Donegal, 1630. [Donegal Muster Roll]

ARNOT, Sir CHARLES, Captain of Home of the Heugh's Regiment at Carrickfergus on 9 September 1642. [DS#336]

ARNOT, CHARLES, Captain of Major General Robert Monro's Regiment in Carrickfergus on 9 September 1642. [DS#329]

ARRELL, JOHN, mustered with sword and snaphance in the barony of Raphoe, County Donegal, 1630. [Donegal Muster Roll]

AYRE, WILLIAM, in the barony of Magheraboy, County Fermanagh, 1631. [Fermanagh Muster Roll]

BAILLIE, JAMES, a minister at Glasserton, Angus, then in Clandavoch, Ireland, by 1702. [NAS.RS35.10.349]

BAILLIE, PHIL., a witness in Dungannon, County Tyrone, 8 March 1667. [CSPIre]

BAILLIE, Captain, an assignment dated 1672. [NAS.RH15.91.39]

BAIRD, ANDREW, in Anlow, County Londonderry, 9 August 1666. [NAS.RH15.91.40]

BAIRD, ROBERT, in Anlow, County Londonderry, 9 August 1666. [NAS.RH15.91.40]

BALFOUR, ALEXANDER, in the barony of Magherasterhana and Clankeilly, County Fermanagh, 1631. [Fermanagh Muster Roll]

BALFOUR, JAMES, in the barony of Magherasterhana and Clankeilly, County Fermanagh, 1631. [Fermanagh Muster Roll]

BALLENDINE, JAMES, Captain Major of the Lifeguard of Horse at Carrickfergus on 10 September 1642. [DS#339]

BALMAND, ANDREW, mustered unarmed in the barony of Raphoe, County Donegal, 1630. [Donegal Muster Roll]

BALMANNER, ALEXANDER, mustered with a sword and
snaphance in the barony of Raphoe, Donegal, 1630.
[Donegal Muster Roll]

BALMANNER, ANDREW, mustered with a sword and
snaphance in the barony of Raphoe, Donegal, 1630.
[Donegal Muster Roll]

BANNERMAN, ALEXANDER, Captain of Lord Sinclair's
Regiment in Newry on 28 September 1642. [DS#337]

BANNERMAN, or FORBES, JEAN, born 1616, died 7
September 1681. [St Anne's gravestone, Ballyshannon,
County Donegal]

BARBOR, JOHN, mustered with a sword and callener in the
barony of Raphoe, County Donegal, 1630. [Donegal
Muster Roll]

BARCLAY, ALEXANDER, Major of the Earl of Glencairn's
Regiment in Carrickfergus on 9 September 1642.
[DS#331]

BARCLAY, GEORGE, Major of Major General Robert
Monro's Regiment in Carrickfergus on 9 September
1642. [DS#329]

BARCLAY, JOHN, died in Ireland, probate 1602 PCC

BARCLAY, JEAN, wife of Daniel Couper in Ballchasker,
Ireland, 14 August 1624. [NAS.RS11.3.133]

BARCLAY, PETER, in Strangford, 1630. [see Janet
Archibald's testament, confirmed 23 March 1630,
Glasgow. NAS.CC9]

BARCLAY, WILLIAM, a burgess of Irvine, Ayrshire, and a
Baillie of Bangor, County Down, husband of Janet
McDowall, daughter of Uchted McDowell of Kilsay,
Provost of Bangor, 1616. [AG.VII.201]

BARLEY, ROBERT, mustered with a sword and snaphance in the barony of Raphoe, County Donegal, 1630. [Donegal Muster Roll]

BARR, WILLIAM, mustered with sword and halbert in the barony of Raphoe, County Donegal, 1630. [Donegal Muster Roll]

BARRON, ANDREW, in Killelagh, County Down,, 1671. [NAS.RH15.91.38]

BARSKENNY, HUGH, mustered with sword and pike in the barony of Raphoe, County Donegal, 1630. [Donegal Muster Roll]

BAXTER, JOHN, mustered unarmed in the barony of Raphoe, County Donegal, 1630. [Donegal Muster Roll]

BAYLEY, the widow, a tenant of William Conyngham in Armagh, 1683. [DP]

BEATTIE, ADAM, in the barony of Magherasterhana and Clankeilly, County Fermanagh, 1631. [Fermanagh Muster Roll]

BEATTIE, ARTHUR, in the barony of Magherasterhana and Clankeilly, County Fermanagh, 1631. [Fermanagh Muster Roll]

BEATTIE, DAVID, in the barony of Magherasterhana and Clankeilly, County Fermanagh, 1631. [Fermanagh Muster Roll]

BEATTIE, JOHN, mustered unarmed in the barony of Raphoe, County Donegal, 1630. [Donegal Muster Roll]

BEATTIE, MATTHEW, in the barony of Magherasterhana and Clankeilly, County Fermanagh, 1631. [Fermanagh Muster Roll]

BEATTIE, RICHARD, in the barony of Magheraboy, County Fermanagh, 1631. [Fermanagh Muster Roll]

BEATTIE, THOMAS, in the barony of Magheraboy, County
Fermanagh, 1631. [Fermanagh Muster Roll]

BEATTIE, WILLIAM, in the barony of Magherasterhana and
Clankeilly, County Fermanagh, 1631. [Fermanagh
Muster Roll]

BELL, ANDREW, Major of the Earl of Eglinton's Regiment
in Bangor on 9 September 1642. [DS#333]

BELL, Lieutenant ANDREW, a will dated 1671.
[PRONI.T640/115]

BELL, JOHN, mustered with a sword in the barony of
Raphoe, County Donegal, 1630. [Donegal Muster Roll]

BELL, PATRICK, in the parish of Raphoe, County Donegal,
1665. [HTR]

BELL, THOMAS, a merchant in Bridge Street, 23 April 1678.
[NAS.RH15.91.40]

BELL, ..., in the barony of Magheraboy, County
Fermanagh, 1631. [Fermanagh Muster Roll]

BIGGAR, JOSEPH, born 1676, a merchant from Belfast
aboard the Friendship of Belfast, was captured by pirates
off the coast of Virginia in 1700. [NA.HCA1.26.14]

BINNIE, JAMES, in the barony of Magherstefeny (?), County
Fermanagh, 1631. [Fermanagh Muster Roll]

BINNING, JAMES, a letter dated 1649. [NAS.RH15.91.39]

BIRSBANE, WILLIAM, Captain of the Earl of Eglinton's
Regiment in Bangor on 9 September 1642. [DS#333]

BIRSE, JOHN, in the barony of Magheraboy, County
Fermanagh, 1631. [Fermanagh Muster Roll]

BLACK, HENRY, in the barony of Magheraboy, County
Fermanagh, 1631. [Fermanagh Muster Roll]

BLACK, JOHN, in the barony of Magheraboy, County Fermanagh, 1631. [Fermanagh Muster Roll]

BLACK, NICHOLAS, an Irish minister, a refugee in Kirkcaldy, Fife, 1643. [PBK.236]

BLACK, ROBERT, in the barony of Magheraboy, County Fermanagh, 1631. [Fermanagh Muster Roll]

BLAIN, MICHAEL, in the county of Bannach, Ireland, 10 March 1674. [Laing#2728]

BLAINE, PATRICK, of Auchencrag, in the parish of Raphoe, County Donegal, 1665. [HTR]

BLAIR, BRYCE, Captain of the Earl of Eglinton's Regiment in Bangor on 9 September 1642. [DS#333]

BLAIR, GEORGE, a drummer, in Dungiven, County Londonderry, 1630. [Dungiven Muster Roll]

BLAIR, JAMES, Captain of the Earl of Leven's Regiment in Carrickfergus, 9 September 1642. [DS#328]

BLAIR, JOHN, mustered with a sword in the barony of Raphoe, Donegal, 1630. [Donegal Muster Roll]

BLAIR, JOHN, of 'Maghrisollus', in the parish of Raphoe, County Donegal, 1665. [HTR]

BLAIR, ROBERT, Captain of the Earl of Leven's Regiment in Carrickfergus, 9 September 1642. [DS#328]

BLAIR, THOMAS, a receipt dated 1662. [NAS.RH15.91.40]

BLAIR, Sir WILLIAM, Captain of Major General Robert Monro's Regiment in Carrickfergus on 9 September 1642. [DS#329]

BLANE, THOMAS, mustered in the barony of Raphoe, County Donegal, 1630. [Donegal Muster Roll]

BORTHWICK, THOMAS, Captain of the Earl of Lindsay's Regiment at Carrickfergus in September 1642. [DS#334]

BORTHWICK, WILLIAM, Major of the Earl of Lindsay's Regiment at Carrickfergus in September 1642. [DS#334]

BOSTON, ADAM, in the parish of Kilwaghter, 1652. [NAS.GD154.514]

BOSWELL, JAMES, a merchant in Edinburgh supplying the Scots army in Ireland, 1640s. [NAS.PA7.3.4A; PA7.3.17, 18]

BOSWELL, JOHN, a gentleman who died in Ireland, probate 1692 PCC

BOYD, ADAM, in the Routt or the Glens of Antrim, a witness in 1661. [CSP.Ire.1661]

BOYD, Colonel DAVID, in County Down, 1610. [Laing#1582]

BOYD, GEORGE, Captain of the Earl of Eglinton's Regiment in Bangor on 9 September 1642. [DS#333]

BOYD, JOHN, in Dungiven, County Londonderry, 1630. [Dungiven Muster Roll]

BOYD, ROBERT, mustered with a sword in the barony of Raphoe, County Donegal, 1630. [Donegal Muster Roll]

BOYD, ROBERT, in Ireland, 1669. [NAS.AC7.4]

BOYD, ROBERT, supercargo of the Northbore of Londonderry in 1705. [CalSPDom.SP42/120/61]

BOYD, ROBERT, a merchant in Londonderry, 1708. [NAS.AC9.298]

BOYD, THOMAS, sometime provost of Irvine, residing in Ireland, husband of Elizabeth Smeyton widow of Alexander Campbell minister of Stevenston, disposed of property in Irvine on 3 August 1616. [AG.VII.38]

BOYD, THOMAS, in Dungiven, County Londonderry, 1630. [Dungiven Muster Roll]

BOYD, THOMAS, a merchant and owner of the Mary of Dublin, a prisoner in Dublin, was pardoned on 19 February 1666. [CSPIre]

BOYD, WILLIAM, mustered unarmed in the barony of Raphoe, County Donegal, 1630. [Donegal Muster Roll]

BOYES, WILLIAM, mustered unarmed in the barony of Raphoe, County Donegal, 1630. [Donegal Muster Roll]

BOYLE, JAMES, aged 52, a witness, 26 August 1656. [NAS.RH15.91.38]

BOYLE, JANET, a servant in Gallanagh, parish of Urney, County Tyrone, 1660. [Poll Tax Returns]

BOYLL, ROBERT, mustered with a sword in the barony of Raphoe, Donegal, 1630. [Donegal Muster Roll]

BREADY, JAMES, in the parish of Raphoe, County Donegal, 1665. [HTR]

BRECKINRIDGE, ALEXANDER, born 1641, died 29 August 1689. [Clogher Cathedral gravestone]

BRECKINRIDGE, JOHN, late of Ballymacan, born 1672, died 17 February 1721, his wife Barbara born 1679, died 24 August 1720. [Clogher Cathedral gravestone]

BREDENE, ARCHIBALD, mustered in the barony of Raphoe, County Donegal, 1630. [Donegal Muster Roll]

BRICE, JAMES, Captain of the Earl of Eglinton's Regiment in Bangor on 9 September 1642. [DS#333]

BRICE, ROBERT, an account of rent, post 1661. [PRONI.T640/91]

BROCK, JAMES, in the barony of Magheraboy, County
Fermanagh, 1631. [Fermanagh Muster Roll]

BROCK, JOHN, in the barony of Magheraboy, County
Fermanagh, 1631. [Fermanagh Muster Roll]

BROCK, WILLIAM, in the barony of Magheraboy, County
Fermanagh, 1631. [Fermanagh Muster Roll]

BROK, RICHARD, of Dunkinmick, leased lands in
Glencorme from Archibald Edmonstone of Braidisland,
on 15 July 1627. [NAS.GD97.Sec.1/388]

BROOKE, ARCHIBALD, rector of Baltragh, 12 November
1630. [PRONI.T640/25]

BROWN, ALEXANDER, in Inshoan, Donegal, son of
Alexander Brown in Iles, 15 June 1627.
[NAS.RS11.4.67]

BROWN, ALEXANDER, in Dungiven, County Londonderry,
1630. [Dungiven Muster Roll]

BROWN, JAMES, mustered unarmed in the barony of
Raphoe, County Donegal, 1630. [Donegal Muster Roll]

BROWN, JOHN, in the barony of Magherasterhana and
Clankeilly, County Fermanagh, 1631. [Fermanagh
Muster Roll]

BROWNE, GEORGE, in the parish of Raphoe, County
Donegal, 1665. [HTR]

BROWNE, JOHN, mustered in the barony of Raphoe, County
Donegal, 1630. [Donegal Muster Roll]

BROWNE, MARY, daughter of John Browne from Edinburgh
was baptised in Blaris, Lisburn, County Down, on 28
September 1678. [Blaris Parish Register]

BROWNE, THOMAS, mustered unarmed in the barony of
Raphoe, County Donegal, 1630. [Donegal Muster Roll]

BRUCE, ROBERT, in the parish of Killowen, County Londonderry, leased lands in the parish of Dunboe, County Londonderry, from John, Lord Kirkcudbright, on 18 March 1655. [NAS.RH15.91.32][PRONI.T640/60]

BRUCE, WILLIAM, Captain of the Campbell of Lawers Regiment at Temple Patrick on 10 September 1642. [DS#335]

BRYDEN, ANDREW, Captain of Major General Robert Monro's Regiment in Carrickfergus on 9 September 1642. [DS#329]

BRYDEN, ..., son of Hugh Bryden in Port Ballintray, Ireland, a witness in Irvine, 1619. [AG.IV.111]

BUCHANAN, ALEXANDER, mustered with a sword in the barony of Raphoe, County Donegal, 1630. [Donegal Muster Roll]

BUCHANAN, GEORGE, of Cullaghy, in the parish of Raphoe, County Donegal, 1665. [HTR]

BUCHANAN, JOHN, mustered with a sword in the barony of Raphoe, County Donegal, 1630. [Donegal Muster Roll]

BUCHANAN, JOHN, mustered unarmed in the barony of Raphoe, County Donegal, 1630. [Donegal Muster Roll]

BUCHANAN, JOHN, a merchant in Dublin, 1684. [NAS.RH1.2.797]

BUCHANAN, PATRICK, mustered with sword and snaphance in the barony of Raphoe, County Donegal, 1630. [Donegal Muster Roll]

BUCHANAN, ROBERT, mustered with a sword in the barony of Raphoe, County Donegal, 1630. [Donegal Muster Roll]

BURNETT, JOHN, in the parish of Kilwaghter, 1652. [NAS.GD154.514]

BURNSIDE, ROBERT, in the parish of Raphoe, County Donegal, 1665. [HTR]

BYERS, DAVID, in the barony of Magheraboy, County Fermanagh, 1631. [Fermanagh Muster Roll]

BYRES, ..., master of the Sara of Belfast, 1721. [NAS.AC9.757]

CAIRNS, DAVID, mustered unarmed in the barony of Raphoe, County Donegal, 1630. [Donegal Muster Roll]

CAIRNS, THOMAS, mustered unarmed in the barony of Raphoe, County Donegal, 1630. [Donegal Muster Roll]

CAIRNS, THOMAS, the younger, mustered unarmed in the barony of Raphoe, County Donegal, 1630. [Donegal Muster Roll]

CALDWELL, CATHERINE, wife of John Osburne, in Bert, Donegal, 29 December 1631. [NAS.RS11.5.215]

CALDWELL, JAMES, in the parish of Raphoe, County Donegal, 1665. [HTR]

CALDWELL, ROBERT, in the parish of Raphoe, County Donegal, 1665. [HTR]

CALDWELL, WILLIAM, in the parish of Raphoe, County Donegal, 1665. [HTR]

CALDWELL, WILLIAM, and family, from the parish of Dunboe, emigrated to New England in 1718. [PRONI.D673/49]

CALLY, ARCHIBALD, in Dungiven, County Londonderry, 1630. [Dungiven Muster Roll]

CALWELL, JOHN, mustered with a sword in the barony of Raphoe, County Donegal, 1630. [Donegal Muster Roll]

CALWELL, ROBERT, in County Fermanagh, 1631. [Fermanagh Muster Roll]

CALWELL, WILLIAM, mustered with sword and pike in the barony of Raphoe, County Donegal, 1630. [Donegal Muster Roll]

CAMPBELL, ARCHIBALD, mustered with a sword in the barony of Raphoe, County Donegal, 1630. [Donegal Muster Roll]

CAMPBELL, ARCHIBALD, Captain of the Campbell of Lawers Regiment at Temple Patrick on 10 September 1642. [DS#335]

CAMPBELL, COLIN, Major of the Campbell of Lawers Regiment at Temple Patrick on 10 September 1642. [DS#335]

CAMPBELL, COLIN, Captain of the Marquis of Argyll's Regiment at Dunluce on 16 November 1642. [DS#338]

CAMPBELL, DOUGALL, in Belfast, son of Alexander Campbell a merchant in Edinburgh, a letter dated 1699. [NAS.RH15.14.67]

CAMPBELL, DUNCAN, mustered with a sword in the barony of Raphoe, County Donegal, 1630. [Donegal Muster Roll]

CAMPBELL, Sir DUNCAN, of Auchinbreck, Lieutenant Colonel of the Marquis of Argyll's Regiment at Dunluce on 16 November 1642. [DS#338]

CAMPBELL, DUNCAN, of Dunans, Captain of the Marquis of Argyll's Regiment at Dunluce on 16 November 1642. [DS#338]

CAMPBELL, DUNCAN, of Inverliver, Captain of the Marquis of Argyll's Regiment at Dunluce on 16 November 1642. [DS#338]

CAMPBELL, JAMES, a mariner from Dingle, County Kerry, who died aboard HMS Ruby, probate 1696 PCC

CAMPBELL, JANET, wife of John Peebles of Pethirland, parish of Ballimoney, Ireland, 15 November 1632. [NAS.RS11.5.327]

CAMPBELL, JOHN, mustered with sword and pike in the barony of Raphoe, County Donegal, 1630. [Donegal Muster Roll]

CAMPBELL, JOHN, a witness, 1630. [NAS.RH15.91.38]

CAMPBELL, JOHN, Captain of the Marquis of Argyll's Regiment at Ballycastle on 17 November 1642. [DS#338]

CAMPBELL, JOHN, of Glen McQuein, in the parish of Raphoe, County Donegal, 1665. [HTR]

CAMPBELL, JOHN 'Splayfoot', a prisoner in Carrickfergus, suspected of complicity in the murder of Archbishop Sharp, 1685. [NAS.NRAS.1255.130]

CAMPBELL, MATTHEW, Captain of the Marquis of Argyll's Regiment at Ballymoney on 18 November 1642. [DS#338]

CAMPBELL, Sir MUNGO, Colonel of the Campbell of Lawers' Regiment at Temple Patrick on 10 September 1642. [DS#335]

CAMPBELL, PATRICK, a robber in County Mayo, who was ordered to surrender or be declared a rebel on 29 April 1669. [CSPIre]

CAMPBELL, ROBERT, mustered unarmed in the barony of Raphoe, County Donegal, 1630. [Donegal Muster Roll]

CAMPBELL, ROBERT, Presbyterian minister in Ray, died 1722, a letter dated Londonderry 31 August 1674. [NLS.Wod.Fol.XXVI/4136]

CAMPBELL, WILLIAM, Major of the Marquis of Argyll's Regiment at Dunluce on 16 November 1642. [DS#338]

CAMPBELL, ..., in Londonderry, 1704. [NAS.AC10.9]

CARMICHAEL, GEORGE, mustered with a sword and pike in the barony of Raphoe, County Donegal, 1630. [Donegal Muster Roll]

CARMICHAEL, JAMES, mustered with a sword and snaphance in the barony of Raphoe, County Donegal, 1630. [Donegal Muster Roll]

CARMICHAEL, WILLIAM, mustered with a sword in the barony of Raphoe, County Donegal, 1630. [Donegal Muster Roll]

CARMICHAEL, WILLIAM, mustered with a sword and snaphance in the barony of Raphoe, County Donegal, 1630. [Donegal Muster Roll]

CARMICHAEL, WILLIAM, Captain of the Earl of Leven's Regiment in Carrickfergus, 9 September 1642. [DS#328]

CARMOUTH, JOHN, mustered with a sword in the barony of Raphoe, County Donegal, 1630. [Donegal Muster Roll]

CARR, ALEXANDER, in the barony of Magheraboy, County Fermanagh, 1631. [Fermanagh Muster Roll]

CARR, JOHN, in the barony of Magheraboy, County Fermanagh, 1631. [Fermanagh Muster Roll]

CARR, WALTER, mustered with a sword and calloner in the barony of Raphoe, County Donegal, 1630. [Donegal Muster Roll]

CARSAN, JOHN, in the parish of Raphoe, County Donegal, 1665. [HTR]

CARSAN, RICHARD, mustered with a sword in the barony of Raphoe, County Donegal, 1630. [Donegal Muster Roll]

CARSAN, RICHARD, in the parish of Raphoe, County Donegal, 1665. [HTR]

CARSKADYNE, JAMES, mustered with sword in the barony of Raphoe, County Donegal, 1630. [Donegal Muster Roll]

CARUTH, JOHN, in the parish of Raphoe, County Donegal, 1665. [HTR]

CASSEN, JOHN, in County Down, 1610. [Laing#1582]

CATHCART, JOHN, in Romillan, Donegal, 2 July 1628. [NAS.RS11.4.256]

CAUGHLAN, ROBERT, in the parish of Raphoe, County Donegal, 1665. [HTR]

CAYE, THOMAS, in the parish of Kilwaghter, 1652. [NAS.GD154.514]

CHARLETON, Lieutenant JOHN, of Killishandra, 1669. [NAS.AC7.4]

CHIRNSIDE, DAVID, Captain of Lord Sinclair's Regiment in Newry on 28 September 1642. [DS#337]

CHIRNSIDE, GEORGE, in the barony of Magheraboy, County Fermanagh, 1631. [Fermanagh Muster Roll]

CHIRNSIDE, JOHN, in the barony of Magherasterhana and Clankeilly, County Fermanagh, 1631. [Fermanagh Muster Roll]

CHRISTALL, ROBERT, in the barony of Magherstefeny (?), County Fermanagh, 1631. [Fermanagh Muster Roll]

CLARKE, THOMAS, mustered with a sword in the barony of Raphoe, County Donegal, 1630. [Donegal Muster Roll]

CLEVIE, JOHN, born 6 September 1644 son of John Clevie in Old Aberdeen, graduated Master of Arts from King's College, Aberdeen, on 30 April 1663, was admitted as a burgess of Aberdeen on 19 February 1674, Episcopal minister of Newhills, Aberdeenshire, Clerk of the Synod, deposed on 1 July 1695, moved to Ireland. [F.3.63]

CLUGSTON, ROBERT, in Newton, Ireland, 1645. [NLS.Wod.Fol.XXV/52]

CLYDE, ROBERT, formerly in Ballehamlin, 1659. [NAS.RH15.91.38]

COCHRANE, BRYCE, Captain of the Earl of Glencairn's Regiment in Carrickfergus on 9 September 1642. [DS#332]

COCHRANE, JOHN, mustered with a sword and a pike in the barony of Raphoe, County Donegal, 1630. [Donegal Muster Roll]

COCHRANE, JOHN, mustered with a sword in the barony of Raphoe, County Donegal, 1630. [Donegal Muster Roll]

COCHRANE, ROBERT, mustered with a sword in the barony of Raphoe, County Donegal, 1630. [Donegal Muster Roll]

COCHRANE, ROBERT, [1], in the parish of Raphoe, County Donegal, 1665. [HTR]

COCHRANE, ROBERT, [2], in the parish of Raphoe, County Donegal, 1665. [HTR]

COCHRANE, ROBERT, a tenant of William Conyngham in Armagh, 1683. [DP/Lenox-Conyngham pp]

COCHRANE, WILLIAM, Major of Home of the Heugh's Regiment at Carrickfergus on 9 September 1642. [DS#336]

COCHRANE, WILLIAM, mustered with a sword in the barony of Raphoe, County Donegal, 1630. [Donegal Muster Roll]

COCHRANE, Sir WILLIAM, of Cowdoun, to Ireland in 1645. [NAS.PA7.3.102]

COLQUHOUN, ADAM, mustered unarmed in the barony of Raphoe, County Donegal, 1630. [Donegal Muster Roll]

COLQUHOUN, ANDREW, mustered with sword and pike in the barony of Raphoe, County Donegal, 1630. [Donegal Muster Roll]

COLQUHOUN, JAMES, mustered with sword and pike in the barony of Raphoe, County Donegal, 1630. [Donegal Muster Roll]

COLT, JAMES, a receipt dated 1662. [NAS.RH15.91.40]

COLVILL, Dr ALEXANDER, in Ballgorin, County Antrim, a bond dated 1663. [PRONI.T640/96]

CON, WILLIAM, in the parish of Kilwaghter, 1652. [NAS.GD154.514]

CONN, HECTOR, mustered with a sword in the barony of Raphoe, County Donegal, 1630. [Donegal Muster Roll]

CONYNGHAM, ALEXANDER, in the parish of Raphoe, County Donegal, 1665. [HTR]

CONYNGHAM, CUTHBERT, in County Down, 1610. [Laing#1582]

CONYNGHAM, DAVID, mustered with a sword in the barony of Raphoe, Donegal, 1630. [Donegal Muster Roll]

CONYNGHAM, HENRY, of Mount Charles, County Donegal, 20 January 1698. [Laing#2969]

CONYNGHAM, Lieutenant PAUL, a tenant on William Conyngham's lands in County Londonderry, 1683. [DP/Lenox-Conyngham pp]

CONYNGHAM, WALTER, in the parish of Raphoe, County Donegal, 1665. [HTR]

CONYNGHAM, WILLIAM, proprietor of the freehold townland of Ballydrom, County Londonderry, 9 August 1689. [DP/Lenox-Conyngham pp]

CONYNGHAM, WILLIAM, of Lecrum, barony of Boylagh and Bannah, County Donegal, 20 January 1698. [Laing#2969]

COOK, GILBERT, in Ireland, son of John Cook a weaver in Maybole, Ayrshire, 4 July 1619. [NAS.RS11.1.359]

COOKE, HUMPHREY, mustered in the barony of Raphoe, County Donegal, 1630. [Donegal Muster Roll]

COOKE, JOHN, in Limnavaddy, 1615. [NAS.RH15.91.33]

COOPER, ANDREW, merchant in Newport, Ireland, and owner of the Broswell of Newport, Ireland, 1721. [NAS.AC8.260]

CORSAN, WILLIAM, mustered with a sword and snaphance in the barony of Raphoe, County Donegal, 1630. [Donegal Muster Roll]

COULTER, JAMES, in the barony of Magheraboy, County Fermanagh, 1631. [Fermanagh Muster Roll]

COUPAR, JOHN, son of the late Alexander Coupar, letter dated 1649. [NAS.RH15.91.39]

COURTIS, PETER, of Flemington, tanner in County Meath, 1714. [LI#403]

COUTHART, JAMES, a lease dated 29 October 1696. [PRONI.T640/139]

CRAFFORD, DAVID, mustered unarmed in the barony of Raphoe, County Donegal, 1630. [Donegal Muster Roll]

CRAFFORD, DUNCAN, mustered unarmed in the barony of Raphoe, County Donegal, 1630. [Donegal Muster Roll]

CRAFFORD, JAMES, reference, 2 November 1698. [DP]

CRAFFORD, JOHN, in barony of Raphoe, 1630. [Donegal Muster Roll]

CRAFFORD, PATRICK, mustered with sword and pike in the barony of Raphoe, County Donegal, 1630. [Donegal Muster Roll]

CRAFFORD, ROBERT, in barony of Raphoe, 1630. [Donegal Muster Roll]

CRAFFORD, WILLIAM, mustered with sword and pike in the barony of Raphoe, County Donegal, 1630. [Donegal Muster Roll]

CRAGG, STEPHEN, mustered unarmed in the barony of Raphoe, County Donegal, 1630. [Donegal Muster Roll]

CRAGG, THOMAS, in the barony of Magherasterhana and Clankeilly, County Fermanagh, 1631. [Fermanagh Muster Roll]

CRAGG, WILLIAM, mustered unarmed in the barony of Raphoe, County Donegal, 1630. [Donegal Muster Roll]

CRANSTON, THOMAS, mustered with a sword in the barony of Raphoe, County Donegal, 1630. [Donegal Muster Roll]

CRANSTON, THOMAS, in the barony of Magheraboy, County Fermanagh, 1631. [Fermanagh Muster Roll]

CRANSTON, WILLIAM, in the barony of Magheraboy, County Fermanagh, 1631. [Fermanagh Muster Roll]

CRAWFORD, JOHN, in barony of Raphoe, 1630. [Donegal Muster Roll]

CRAWFORD, JOHN, in Dungiven, County Londonderry, 1630. [Dungiven Muster Roll]

CRAWFORD, JOHN, Captain of the Earl of Glencairn's Regiment in Carrickfergus on 9 September 1642. [DS#332]

CRAWFORD, MALCOLM, Captain of the Earl of Glencairn's Regiment in Carrickfergus on 9 September 1642. [DS#332]

CREAGH, JAMES, mustered with sword and snaphance in the barony of Raphoe, County Donegal, 1630. [Donegal Muster Roll]

CREICHTON, ALEXANDER, a witness in Dungannon, County Tyrone, 8 March 1667. [CSPIre]

CREIGHTON, JOHN, in Ireland, was served as heir to his father John Creighton of Achleen and brother of Sir Robert Creighton of Gladsmuir, 18 February 1724. [NAS.S/H]

CREIGHTON, JOHN, mustered in the barony of Raphoe, County Donegal, 1630. [Donegal Muster Roll]

CRICHTON, JOHN, a witness in Dungannon, County Tyrone, 8 March 1667. [CSPIre]

CROYDIE, ROBERT, in Ireland, a debtor of Mungo Graham a merchant burgess of Dumfries, 1631. [NAS.CC5.6.1/252]

CUMMING, ELIZABETH, wife of Robert Smith, refugees from Ireland, in Elgin, Morayshire, 1643. [Elgin KSR]

CUNNINGHAM, ALEXANDER, minister of Kirkinver, Donegal, husband of Katherine Murray, 6 July 1621. [NAS.RS11.2.171]

CUNNINGHAM, ALEXANDER, in barony of Raphoe, 1630. [Donegal Muster Roll]

CUNNINGHAM, ALEXANDER, Captain of the Earl of Glencairn's Regiment in Carrickfergus on 9 September 1642. [DS#332]

CUNNINGHAM, ALEXANDER, minister at Kirkinver, County Donegal. 31 May 1643 and 1 November 1659. [NAS.RS11.7.531; RS11.9.478]

CUNNINGHAM, ANDREW, in barony of Raphoe, 1630. [Donegal Muster Roll]

CUNNINGHAM, ARCHIBALD, mustered with a sword in the barony of Raphoe, County Donegal, 1630. [Donegal Muster Roll]

CUNNINGHAM, BERNARD, mustered unarmed in the barony of Raphoe, County Donegal, 1630. [Donegal Muster Roll]

CUNNINGHAM, DAVID, of Heurt, was assigned land in the County of Coleraine by Sir Robert McClellan of Bomby in 1614. [PRONI.T640]

CUNNINGHAM, GEORGE, of Ballyloheristowe, 28 August 1610. [Laing#1582]

CUNNINGHAM, J., witnessed a lease on 17 September 1659. [DP]

CUNNINGHAM, JAMES, in barony of Raphoe, 1630. [Donegal Muster Roll]

CUNNINGHAM, JOHN, a merchant and sometime provost of Newton, County Down, 1640. [HH.80]

CUNNINGHAM, JOHN, a debtor of Sir Robert Maxwell, 1663. [NAS.RH15.91.38D]

CUNNINGHAM, JOHN, a merchant in Londonderry, 1711. [NAS.AC10.103]

CUNNINGHAM, MATTHEW, mustered unarmed in the barony of Raphoe, County Donegal, 1630. [Donegal Muster Roll]

CUNNINGHAM, PATRICK, mustered with a sword in the barony of Raphoe, Donegal, 1630. [Donegal Muster Roll]

CUNNINGHAM, ROBERT, minister of Holywood, Ireland, 12 November 1619. [NAS.RS11.1.379]

CUNNINGHAM, ROBERT, Captain of the Earl of Glencairn's Regiment in Carrickfergus on 9 September 1642. [DS#332]

CUNNINGHAM, ROBERT, an assizeman in Dungannon, County Tyrone, 8 March 1667. [CSPIre]

CUNNINGHAM, THOMAS, a yeoman in the parish of Dunboe, County Londonderry, leased Tiperclair, parish of Dunboe, from John, Lord Kirkcudbright, on 13 August 1655. [NAS.RH15.91.32][PRONI.T640/73]

CUNNINGHAM, THOMAS, a tenant, 1663. [NAS.RH15.91.38C]

CUNNINGHAM, WILLIAM, mustered with sword and pike in barony of Raphoe, 1630. [Donegal Muster Roll]

CUNNINGHAM, WILLIAM, merchant in Articlare, County Londonderry, 22 January 1635. [NAS.RH15.91.61] [PRONI.T640/36]

CUNNINGHAM, WILLIAM, Lieutenant Colonel of the Earl of Glencairn's Regiment in Carrickfergus on 9 September 1642. [DS#331]

CUNNINGHAM, WILLIAM, Captain of the Earl of Glencairn's Regiment in Carrickfergus on 9 September 1642. [DS#331]

CUNNINGHAM, WILLIAM, leased the townland or balliboe of Mullaghmehoagh in the territory of Munterevelinge

Itragh, barony of Dungannon, County Tyrone, from
Andrew Stewart of Tierarly, County Armagh, for 3
years, dated 17 September 1659. [DP]

CUTHBERTSON, WILLIAM, mustered with a sword and
callener in the barony of Raphoe, County Donegal, 1630.
[Donegal Muster Roll]

DALYELL, THOMAS, Captain of Major General Robert
Monro's Regiment in Carrickfergus on 9 September
1642. [DS#329]

DARROCH, JOHN, minister of Kilcalmonell and Kilberry in
Kintire from 1669 to 1681, then a Presbyterian minister
in Glenarm, Ireland, returned to Argyll by 1689. [F.4.58]

DAVEY, WILLIAM, a merchant in Dublin, 1714.
[NAS.AC9.493]

DAVIDSON, JANET, spouse of John Wallace a workman in
Ireland, 10 May 1621. [NAS.RS11.2.155]

DAVIDSON, JANET, spouse of John Wallace a smith in
Maybole, Ayrshire, then in Ireland, 24 November 1635.
[NAS.RS11.6.414]

DAVISON, JOHN, in the parish of Raphoe, County Donegal,
1665. [HTR]

DAVY, BENJAMIN, a merchant in Londonderry, 1720.
[NAS.AC9.675]

DAVY, HUGH, in Londonderry, 1709. [NAS.AC9.332]

DAVY, JAMES, mustered with sword and pike in barony of
Raphoe, 1630. [Donegal Muster Roll]

DAVY, JOHN, mustered unarmed in the barony of Raphoe,
County Donegal, 1630. [Donegal Muster Roll]

DAVY, MUNGO, mustered unarmed in the barony of Raphoe,
County Donegal, 1630. [Donegal Muster Roll]

DAWSON, WALTER, a tenant of William Conyngham in Armagh, 1683. [DP/Lenox-Conyngham pp]

DENNISTON, JAMES, the elder, mustered with a sword in the barony of Raphoe, County Donegal, 1630. [Donegal Muster Roll]

DENNISTON, JOHN, mustered with a sword and snaphance in the barony of Raphoe, County Donegal, 1630. [Donegal Muster Roll]

DENNISTON, ROBERT, mustered unarmed in the barony of Raphoe, County Donegal, 1630. [Donegal Muster Roll]

DICK, HUGH, in the parish of Raphoe, County Donegal, 1665. [HTR]

DICK, JAMES, mustered with a sword and pike in the barony of Raphoe, County Donegal, 1630. [Donegal Muster Roll]

DICK, JAMES, in the parish of Raphoe, County Donegal, 1665. [HTR]

DINGWALL, ROBERT, in Carrownane, parish of Killaraght, County Sligo, 1665. [Hearth Tax Roll]

DIXON, JAMES, in Grangebeg, parish of Templeboy, County Sligo, 1665. [Hearth Tax Roll]

DIXON, WILLIAM, mustered with a sword and calloner in the barony of Raphoe, County Donegal, 1630. [Donegal Muster Roll]

DOD, THOMAS, in Abbeytown, parish of Ballysadare, County Sligo, 1665. [Hearth Tax Roll]

DODD, CHARLES, in Knockbane, parish of Tawnagh, County Sligo, 1665. [Hearth Tax Roll]

DONALDSON, AGNES, born 1648, wife of Robert Kincaid, died 27 May 1718. [Ballykeel, Islandmagee, gravestone]

DOUGLAS, HECTOR, mustered unarmed in the barony of Raphoe, County Donegal, 1630. [Donegal Muster Roll]

DOUGLAS, JOHN, mustered unarmed in the barony of Raphoe, County Donegal, 1630. [Donegal Muster Roll]

DOUGLAS, WILLIAM, mustered with a sword in the barony of Raphoe, County Donegal, 1630. [Donegal Muster Roll]

DOUGLAS, WILLIAM, mustered unarmed in the barony of Raphoe, County Donegal, 1630. [Donegal Muster Roll]

DRENNAN, DAVID, in Anlow, County Londonderry, 9 August 1666. [NAS.RH15.91.40]

DRUMMOND, ALEXANDER, Captain of the Earl of Lothian's Regiment in Carrickfergus on 9 September 1642. [DS#329]

DRUMMOND, JAMES, mustered with a sword in the barony of Raphoe, County Donegal, 1630. [Donegal Muster Roll]

DRUMMOND, JOHN, Captain of the Campbell of Lawers Regiment at Temple Patrick on 10 September 1642. [DS#335]

DRUMMOND, MARGARET, wife of John Hanna in Carrickfergus, 1683. [NAS.RD2/61/299, 301, 303]

DRUMMOND, ROBERT, Captain of the Earl of Lindsay's Regiment at Carrickfergus in September 1642. [DS#334]

DRUMMOND, THOMAS, a non-conformist minister who had been imprisoned for seven years in Lifford gaol, petitioned King Charles II for his release, 1669. [CSPIre]

DRUMMOND, WILLIAM, Captain of Major General Robert Monro's Regiment in Carrickfergus on 9 September 1642. [DS#329]

DRYDEN, DAVID, in the parish of Raphoe, County Donegal, 1665. [HTR]

DRYELAND, HUGH, in the parish of Raphoe, County Donegal, 1665. [HTR]

DUNBAR, PATRICK, mustered unarmed in the barony of Raphoe, County Donegal, 1630. [Donegal Muster Roll]

DUNCAN, ALEXANDER, in Dungiven, County Londonderry, 1630. [Dungiven Muster Roll]

DUNCAN, JAMES, mustered unarmed in the barony of Raphoe, County Donegal, 1630. [Donegal Muster Roll]

DUNCAN, JOHN, senior, in the parish of Raphoe, County Donegal, 1665. [HTR]

DUNCAN, JOHN, in the parish of Raphoe, County Donegal, 1665. [HTR]

DUNCAN, WILLIAM, in the barony of Magherasterhana and Clankeilly, County Fermanagh, 1631. [Fermanagh Muster Roll]

DUNCAN, WILLIAM, in Dungiven, County Londonderry, 1630. [Dungiven Muster Roll]

DUNDAS, JAMES, in the barony of Magheraboy, County Fermanagh, 1631. [Fermanagh Muster Roll]

DUNLOP, ALEXANDER, in the parish of Kilwaghter, 1652. [NAS.GD154.514]

DUNLOP, ALEXANDER, in Anlow, County Londonderry, 9 August 1666. [NAS.RH15.91.40]

DUNLOP, JOHN, mustered with a sword and snaphance in the barony of Raphoe, County Donegal, 1630. [Donegal Muster Roll]

DUNLOP, PATRICK, mustered with sword and pike in the barony of Raphoe, County Donegal, 1630. [Donegal Muster Roll]

DUNLOP, WILLIAM, of Craig, Kilmaurs, Ayrshire, had "tenants in Ireland", according to the testament of his wife Jean Campbell which was confirmed in Glasgow on 15 March 1621. [NAS.CC9]

DUNLOP, WILLIAM, mustered with sword and pike in the barony of Raphoe, County Donegal, 1630. [Donegal Muster Roll]

DUNLOP, WILLIAM, mustered with a sword in the barony of Raphoe, Donegal, 1630. [Donegal Muster Roll]

DUNLOP, WILLIAM, mustered with a sword and pike in the barony of Raphoe, County Donegal, 1630. [Donegal Muster Roll]

DUNLOP, WILLIAM, in Anlow, County Londonderry, 9 August 1666. [NAS.RH15.91.40]

DUNN, ANDREW, mustered unarmed in the barony of Raphoe, County Donegal, 1630. [Donegal Muster Roll]

DUNWOODIE, WILLIAM, in the barony of Magherasterhana and Clankeilly, County Fermanagh, 1631. [Fermanagh Muster Roll]

DURHAM, JAMES, Captain of Home of the Heugh's Regiment at Carrickfergus on 9 September 1642. [DS#336]

EDGAR, JOHN, mustered unarmed in the barony of Raphoe, County Donegal, 1630. [Donegal Muster Roll]

EDMONSTONE, ANNA HELENA, of Broadisland, County Antrim, widow of Archibald Edmonstone, and sister and heir of Walter Scott the younger, gentleman, or heir to Colonel Walter Scott senior, on the first part, and Sir Robert Adair of Ballymenoch, son and heir of the said Anna Helena Edmonstone on the second part, James

Montgomery of Rosemount, County Down, on the third
part, and Robert Dollay of Dublin and his son Alexander
Dollay on the fourth and fifth parts, respecting the lands
of Wauchton in Scotland. Robert Montgomery was
married to Elizabeth, eldest daughter of the said
Archibald, and Anna Helena, his youngest daughter was
married to the said Alexander Dollay. Agreement dated
23 October 1696. [NAS.GD97.Sec.1/576]

EDMONSTONE, ARCHIBALD, of Braidisland, granted
power of attorney to his brother James Edmonstone to
uplift rents of Glenchartie, 18 October 1626.
[NAS.GD97.Sec.1/384]

EDMONSTONE, ARCHIBALD, son of the late William
Edmonstone of Braidisland, County Antrim, letters dated
27 February 1627. [NAS.GD97.Sec.1/385]

EDMONSTONE, JAMES, of Ballibantie, 1622.
[NAS.GD97.Sec.1/377]

EDMONSTONE, JAMES, of Ballinbandro, Braidisland,
Ireland, was granted land in Stirlingshire, 26 June 1627.
[Laing#1993]

EDMONSTONE, JAMES, a witness to a tack or lease, 15
July 1627. [NAS.GD97.Sec.1/388]

EDMONSTONE, JOHN, a witness to a tack or lease, 15 July
1627. [NAS.GD97.Sec.1/388]

EDMONSTONE, WILLIAM, of Braidisland, County Antrim,
subleased the lands of Ballytemple, Ballybley, etc. to
Janet .... wife of Robert, Bishop of Down, and John
Echlin of the College of St Andrews, 6 September 1622;
on 16 October 1623 he leased half of Gray Abbey.
[NAS.GD97.Sec.1/376/378]

EDMONSTONE, WILLIAM, of Braid Island, and William
Houston of Ballymenach, agreed to divide Glenachertie
which had been acquired from William Adair if Kinhilt,
18 May 1626. [NAS.GD97.Sec.1/383]

EDWARD, JOHN, mustered with a sword in the barony of Raphoe, County Donegal, 1630. [Donegal Muster Roll]

EDWARD, PATRICK, mariner of the Broswell of Newport, Ireland, 1721. [NAS.AC8.260]

ELLIOT, ANDREW, a chapman from Glen Wherry, Conyer, County Antrim, who died in Tedbury, Gloucestershire, probate 1695 PCC

ELLIOT, GEORGE, mustered unarmed in the barony of Raphoe, County Donegal, 1630. [Donegal Muster Roll]

ELLIOT, JOHN, in the barony of Magheraboy, County Fermanagh, 1631. [Fermanagh Muster Roll]

ELLIOT, MARTIN, in the barony of Magheraboy, County Fermanagh, 1631. [Fermanagh Muster Roll]

ELLIOT, WILLIAM, mustered in the barony of Raphoe, County Donegal, 1630. [Donegal Muster Roll]

ELLIOT, WILLIAM, in the barony of Magheraboy, County Fermanagh, 1631. [Fermanagh Muster Roll]

ELPHINSTONE, ANDREW, mustered unarmed in the barony of Raphoe, County Donegal, 1630. [Donegal Muster Roll]

ELPHINSTONE, MICHAEL, Captain of Home of the Heugh's Regiment at Carrickfergus on 9 September 1642. [DS#336]

ELPHINSTONE, SIMON, mustered unarmed in the barony of Raphoe, County Donegal, 1630. [Donegal Muster Roll]

ELPHINSTONE, THOMAS, mustered with a sword in the barony of Raphoe, County Donegal, 1630. [Donegal Muster Roll]

ENGLISH, JOHN, son of John English from Edinburgh, was baptised in Blaris, Lisburn, County Down, on 31 March 1672. [Blaris Parish Register]

ERSKIN, GEORGE, 1603. [NAS.GD305.1.129/9]

ERVIN, JANET, born 1627, wife of Archibald Ervin of Blessingborn, died 22 May 1682. [Clogher Cathedral gravestone]

ESPEY, HUGH, from Belfast, a merchant in Kirkwall, Orkney, in 1679. [NAS.AC7.75]

EWART, JAMES, in the barony of Magheraboy, County Fermanagh, 1631. [Fermanagh Muster Roll]

EWART, JOHN, from Kirkcudbright, a freeholder in Ulster, 1620s. [NAS.RH15.91.33]

EWART, PATRICK, in the barony of Magheraboy, County Fermanagh, 1631. [Fermanagh Muster Roll]

EWING, FYNDLAY, mustered with a sword and snaphance in the barony of Raphoe, County Donegal, 1630. [Donegal Muster Roll]

EWING, WILLIAM, in the parish of Raphoe, County Donegal, 1665. [HTR]

FAIRIS, JOHN, in Killeleagh, an account dated 12 November 1672. [NAS.RH15.91.39]

FALCONER, HENRY, master of the 60 ton Martine of Dublin, 1715. [MAS.AC13.1.151]

FARQUHAR, JOHN, in the barony of Magherasterhana and Clankeilly, County Fermanagh, 1631. [Fermanagh Muster Roll]

FENTON, JAMES, son of William Fenton minister at Carnecastle, County Antrim, 9 June 1626. [NAS.RS11.3.574/581]

FENTON, WILLIAM, son of William Fenton minister at Carnecastle, County Antrim, 9 June 1626. [NAS.RS11.3.574/581]

FERGUSON, ANDREW, in the parish of Raphoe, County Donegal, 1665. [HTR]

FERGUSON, JAMES, mustered with a sword and snaphance in the barony of Raphoe, County Donegal, 1630. [Donegal Muster Roll]

FERGUSON, WILLIAM, mustered with a sword and snaphance in the barony of Raphoe, County Donegal, 1630. [Donegal Muster Roll]

FERGUSON, WILLIAM, in the barony of Magherasterhana and Clankeilly, County Fermanagh, 1631. [Fermanagh Muster Roll]

FINLAY, ARTHUR, mustered with sword in the barony of Raphoe, County Donegal, 1630. [Donegal Muster Roll]

FINLAY, JAMES, in Dungiven, County Londonderry, 1630. [Dungiven Muster Roll]

FINLAY, JAMES, in the parish of Raphoe, County Donegal, 1665. [HTR]

FISHER, JAMES, a merchant in Londonderry, 1663. [NAS.RH15.91.40][PRONI.T640/97]

FISHER, JOHN, mustered with sword and snaphance in the barony of Raphoe, County Donegal, 1630. [Donegal Muster Roll]

FISHER, RICHARD, a burgess of Coleraine, 1659. [CSPIre]

FLEMING, ADAM, mustered with sword and pike in the barony of Raphoe, County Donegal, 1630. [Donegal Muster Roll]

FLEMING, ARCHIBALD, mustered with a sword and musket in the barony of Raphoe, County Donegal, 1630. [Donegal Muster Roll]

FLEMING, GEORGE, in the parish of Raphoe, County Donegal, 1665. [HTR]

FLEMING, GILBERT, mustered unarmed in the barony of Raphoe, County Donegal, 1630. [Donegal Muster Roll]

FLEMING, JOHN, mustered unarmed in the barony of Raphoe, County Donegal, 1630. [Donegal Muster Roll]

FLEMING, JOHN, a witness, 1695. [NAS.RH15.91.39]

FLEMING, JOHN, in Dublin, 1722. [LI#406]

FLEMING, PATRICK, mustered unarmed in the barony of Raphoe, County Donegal, 1630. [Donegal Muster Roll]

FLEMING, WILLIAM, a yeoman in the parish of Imboe, County Londonderry, indenture with John, Lord Kirkcudbright, dated August 1655. [NAS.RH15.91.32]

FORBES, ROBERT, Captain of Major General Robert Monro's Regiment in Carrickfergus on 9 September 1642. [DS#329]

FORBES, THOMAS, in the barony of Magherasterhana and Clankeilly, County Fermanagh, 1631. [Fermanagh Muster Roll]

FORGAN, ANDREW, a tenant in Ardillam, 1663. [NAS.RH15.91.38]

FORREST, CHARLES, in the barony of Magheraboy, County Fermanagh, 1631. [Fermanagh Muster Roll]

FORREST, MALCOLM, of Gartness, in the parish of Raphoe, County Donegal, 1665. [HTR]

FORRESTER, EDWARD, of Baldorg, Scotland, a freeholder in Ulster, 1620s. [NAS.RH15.91.33]

FORRET, JOHN, mustered with a sword in the barony of Raphoe, Donegal, 1630. [Donegal Muster Roll]

FORSYTH, GAVIN, a minister in Londonderry, 1658. [CSA]

FORSYTH, JAMES, mustered unarmed in the barony of Raphoe, County Donegal, 1630. [Donegal Muster Roll]

FORSYTH, ROBERT, in the parish of Raphoe, County Donegal, 1665. [HTR]

FOSTER, JOHN, mustered with sword in the barony of Raphoe, County Donegal, 1630. [Donegal Muster Roll]

FOULD, PATRICK, mustered with a sword in the barony of Raphoe, Donegal, 1630. [Donegal Muster Roll]

FRAME, ARCHIBALD, in the parish of Raphoe, County Donegal, 1665. [HTR]

FRAME, JOHN, his heirs, absent from Strathaven, probably a Covenanting refugee, to Ireland by 1683. [RPCS.VIII.653]

FRAME, THOMAS, of Drumgumerlan, in the parish of Raphoe, County Donegal, 1665. [HTR]

FRASER, HEW, Lieutenant Colonel of Major General Robert Monro's Regiment in Carrickfergus on 9 September 1642. [DS#329]

FRIZELL, GEORGE, in the barony of Magherasterhana and Clankeilly, County Fermanagh, 1631. [Fermanagh Muster Roll]

FRIZELL, JOHN, mustered unarmed in the barony of Raphoe, County Donegal, 1630. [Donegal Muster Roll]

FRIZELL, JOHN, the younger, mustered with sword and pike in the barony of Raphoe, County Donegal, 1630. [Donegal Muster Roll]

FRIZELL, WILLIAM, mustered unarmed in the barony of Raphoe, County Donegal, 1630. [Donegal Muster Roll]

FULLERTON, HENRY, in Balliknock, County Down, 1701. [LI#402]

FULLERTON, SAMUEL, in Killeleagh, County Down, 1663. [PRONI.T640/96]

FULLERTON, WILLIAM, from Kirkcudbright, a freeholder in Ulster, 1620s. [NAS.RH15.91.33]

FULLERTON, WILLIAM, in the Routt or the Glens of Antrim, a witness in 1661. [CSP.Ire.1661]

FULLERTON, WILLIAM, Collector of Portpatrick, an account for a visit to Ireland, 1691. [NAS.E73.113.3]

FULTON, JOHN, mustered with a sword in the barony of Raphoe, County Donegal, 1630. [Donegal Muster Roll]

FULTON, NINIAN, mustered with a sword and snaphance in the barony of Raphoe, County Donegal, 1630. [Donegal Muster Roll]

FULTON, ROBERT, mustered unarmed in the barony of Raphoe, County Donegal, 1630. [Donegal Muster Roll]

FULTON, THOMAS, a Presbyterian minister in Drumachose, died 1688. [NLS.Wod.Fol.xxvi/4136]

GAGE, WILLIAM, in Ardmagilligan, County Londonderry, marriage settlement, 1 March 1623. [PRONI.T640/19]

GALBRAITH, ALEXANDER, mustered with a sword in the barony of Raphoe, County Donegal, 1630. [Donegal Muster Roll]

GALBRAITH, ANN, born 1648, died 3 June 1718. [Clogher Cathedral gravestone]

GALBRAITH, ARCHIBALD, and his wife, gentry in Ardugboy, parish of Donagheady, 1662. [PRONI.T1365/1]

GALBRAITH, CHRISTIAN, a servant in Ardugboy, parish of Donagheady, 1662. [PRONI.T1365/1]

GALBRAITH, ELIZABETH, wife of Francis Perry of Derrygere, born 1715, died 7 November 1733. [Clogher Cathedral gravestone]

GALBRAITH, HUGH, a merchant in Dublin, 1692. [NAS.E41/20]

GALBRAITH, HUMPHREY, a court order re estates in County Londonderry, 29 June 1658. [PRONI.T640/85]

GALBRAITH, JOHN, mustered with a sword in the barony of Raphoe, County Donegal, 1630. [Donegal Muster Roll]

GALBRAITH, MARTIN, mustered with a sword and snaphance in the barony of Raphoe, County Donegal, 1630. [Donegal Muster Roll]

GALBRAITH, ROBERT, a gentleman in Dublin, 1688. [NAS.AC7.9]

GALBRAITH, THOMAS, of Lisnowall, in the parish of Raphoe, County Donegal, 1665. [HTR]

GALBREATH, ANDREW, mustered unarmed in the barony of Raphoe, County Donegal, 1630. [Donegal Muster Roll]

GALT, JOHN, a receipt dated 1662. [NAS.RH15.91.40]

GALT, WILLIAM, a burgess of Coleraine, 1659. [CSPIre]

GAMBLE, ROBERT, in the parish of Raphoe, County Donegal, 1665. [HTR]

GAMBLE, ROBERT, in Londonderry, 1709. [NAS.AC9.332]

GAY, WILLIAM, in Dungiven, County Londonderry, 1630. [Dungiven Muster Roll]

GIBB, DAVID, mustered unarmed in the barony of Raphoe, County Donegal, 1630. [Donegal Muster Roll]

GIBSON, ALEXANDER, mustered with a sword in the barony of Raphoe, County Donegal, 1630. [Donegal Muster Roll]

GIBSON, GABRIEL, in the barony of Magherstefeny (?), County Fermanagh, 1631. [Fermanagh Muster Roll]

GIBSON, GEORGE, in the barony of Magheraboy, County Fermanagh, 1631. [Fermanagh Muster Roll]

GIBSON, HENRY, Captain of the Campbell of Lawers Regiment at Temple Patrick on 10 September 1642. [DS#335]

GIBSON, JOHN, a merchant from Glasgow, in Belfast in 1685. [NAS.JC39.87]

GIBSON, ROBIN, leased part of Gray Abbey lands known as Ballibrier and Ballimainstra from William Edmonstone of Braidisland, 16 October 1623. [NAS.GD97/Sec.1/378]

GILCHRIST, ROBERT, absent from the town of Strathaven, probably a Covenanting refugee, to Ireland by 1683. [RPCS.VIII.653]

GILL, EDWARD, mustered unarmed in the barony of Raphoe, County Donegal, 1630. [Donegal Muster Roll]

GILLIELAND, JOHN, in Dungiven, County Londonderry, 1630. [Dungiven Muster Roll]

GILLIS, JOHN, mustered with sword in the barony of Raphoe, County Donegal, 1630. [Donegal Muster Roll]

GILMOR, ROBERT, an account dated 15 September 1636. [NAS.RH15.91.39]

GILMORE, DAVID, mustered with sword and musket in the barony of Raphoe, County Donegal, 1630. [Donegal Muster Roll]

GILMORE, ROBERT, in Dungiven, County Londonderry, 1630. [Dungiven Muster Roll]

GILROE, GAVIN, in Dungiven, County Londonderry, 1630. [Dungiven Muster Roll]

GILROY, MATHEW, mustered unarmed in the barony of Raphoe, County Donegal, 1630. [Donegal Muster Roll]

GLASGOW, ARCHIBALD, a minister in Londonderry, March 1658. [CSA]

GLEDSTANES, Captain JAMES, born 1631, died 9 December 1689, his wife Ann Galbraith born 1648 died 3 June 1718. [Clogher Cathedral gravestone]

GLEDSTANES, Captain JAMES, of Roscavey, born 1648, died 10 March 1706. [Clogher Cathedral gravestone]

GLEDSTANES, Captain JOHN, born 1603, died 10 December 1674, his wife Margaret born 1591 died 27 April 1671. [Clogher Cathedral gravestone]

GLEN, GEORGE, in Anlow, County Londonderry, 9 August 1666. [NAS.RH15.91.40]

GLEN, WILLIAM, mustered with a sword in the barony of Raphoe, County Donegal, 1630. [Donegal Muster Roll]

GLEN, WILLIAM, in Anlow, County Londonderry, 9 August 1666. [NAS.RH15.91.40]

GLENDENNING, JOHN. in Anlow, County Londonderry, 9 August 1666. [NAS.RH15.91.40]

GLENDENNING, ROBERT, reference, 2 November 1698. [DP]

GOODFELLOW, JOHN, in the barony of Magheraboy, County Fermanagh, 1631. [Fermanagh Muster Roll]

GOODLATT, THOMAS, an assizeman in Dungannon,
County Tyrone, 8 March 1667. [CSPIre]

GORDON, ANDREW, of Raphoe, in the parish of Raphoe,
County Donegal, 1665. [HTR]

GORDON, GEORGE, Captain of the Earl of Leven's
Regiment in Carrickfergus, 9 September 1642. [DS#328]

GORDON, GILBERT, at Borg, 1616. [NAS.RH15.91.39]

GORDON, JANE, daughter of William Gordon, lord of
Cardoness, parish of Anwoth, Kirkcudbrightshire, was
baptised in Blaris, Lisburn, County Down, on 24 March
1670. [Blaris Parish Register]

GORDON, JAMES, a merchant in Belfast, 1725.
[NAS.AC9.1050, 1071]

GORDON, JANET, wife of William Leslie, refugees from
County Antrim, 1689. [NAS.CH2.635/1/59]

GORDON, JOHN, of Rarsea (?), 1658. [NAS.RH15.91.39]

GORDON, JOHN, a merchant in Belfast, 1728.
[NAS.AC9.1050]

GORDON, Sir ROBERT, was granted 1000 acres in County
Donegal, letters patent dated 2 December 1615.
[Laing#1739]

GORDON,......., in the Routt or the Glens of Antrim, a
witness in 1661. [CSP.Ire.1661]

GOURLAY, B., born 1609, died 19 November 1681. [Clogher
Cathedral gravestone]

GRAHAM, Major ARTHUR, storekeeper at Eniskillen,
County Fermanagh, 1667. [NAS.RH15.91.61]

GRAHAM, CUTHBERT, a tenant of William Conyngham in
Armagh, 1683. [DP/Lenox-Conyngham pp]

GRAHAM, FERGUS, in the barony of Magheraboy, County Fermanagh, 1631. [Fermanagh Muster Roll]

GRAHAM, GEORGE, in the barony of Magheraboy, County Fermanagh, 1631. [Fermanagh Muster Roll]

GRAHAM, JAMES, in the barony of Magherasterhana and Clankeilly, County Fermanagh, 1631. [Fermanagh Muster Roll]

GRAHAM, JAMES, in the barony of Magheraboy, County Fermanagh, 1631. [Fermanagh Muster Roll]

GRAHAM, JOHN, mustered with a sword in the barony of Raphoe, County Donegal, 1630. [Donegal Muster Roll]

GRAHAM, JOHN, in the barony of Magherasterhana and Clankeilly, County Fermanagh, 1631. [Fermanagh Muster Roll]

GRAHAM, JOHN, mariner of the Broswell of Newport, Ireland, 1721. [NAS.AC8.260]

GRAHAM, ROBERT, mustered with sword and pike in the barony of Raphoe, County Donegal, 1630. [Donegal Muster Roll]

GRAHAM, ROBERT, in County Fermanagh, 1631. [Fermanagh Muster Roll]

GRAHAM, ROBERT, in the barony of Magherasterhana and Clankeilly, County Fermanagh, 1631. [Fermanagh Muster Roll]

GRAHAM, SIMON, mustered with a sword in the barony of Raphoe, County Donegal, 1630. [Donegal Muster Roll]

GRAHAM, WILLIAM, in the barony of Magheraboy, County Fermanagh, 1631. [Fermanagh Muster Roll]

GRAHAM, WILLIAM, in Dublin, letter dated 1631. [NAS.GD22.3.589]

GRAHAME, WILLIAM, reference, 2 November 1698. [DP]

GRAY, ARCHIBALD, shipmaster in Donaghadie, 1684.
[RPCS.IX.381]

GRAY, GEORGE, in the parish of Raphoe, County Donegal,
1665. [HTR]

GRAY, JOHN, in the parish of Raphoe, County Donegal,
1665. [HTR]

GRAY, ROBERT, in the parish of Raphoe, County Donegal,
1665. [HTR]

GRAY, THOMAS, mustered with a sword in the barony of
Raphoe, County Donegal, 1630. [Donegal Muster Roll]

GRAY, ..., of Cloghcorr, a widow in the parish of Raphoe,
County Donegal, 1665. [HTR]

GREG, ANDREW, a merchant in Donaghadee, 1692.
[NAS.AC7.9]

GREG, ROBERT, in the parish of Auchlan (?), county
Londonderry, an indenture with Robert Maxwell of
Orchardton, 1646, [NAS.RH15.91.32][PRONI.T640/54]

GREG, WILLIAM, in County Fermanagh, 1631. [Fermanagh
Muster Roll]

GREG, WILLIAM, probably from Donaghadee, a supercargo
on a voyage to the West Indies, 1692. [NAS.AC7.9]

GREGG, JOHN, in County Fermanagh, 1631. [Fermanagh
Muster Roll]

GREGG, ROBERT, in County Fermanagh, 1631. [Fermanagh
Muster Roll]

GREGG, THOMAS, in Anlow, County Londonderry, 9
August 1666. [NAS.RH15.91.40]

GREGORY, Captain ROBERT, reference, 2 November 1698. [DP]

GRIER, DAVID, mustered unarmed in the barony of Raphoe, County Donegal, 1630. [Donegal Muster Roll]

GRIER, GEORGE, in the parish of Raphoe, County Donegal, 1665. [HTR]

GRIER, HUGH, mustered with a sword and a halbert in the barony of Raphoe, County Donegal, 1630. [Donegal Muster Roll]

GRIERSON, JOHN, in Tounfoot of Mulligantoun, afterwards in Ireland, 14 December 1704. [NAS.RS23.7/64]

GRIFFIN, NICHOLAS, in Coleraine, County Londonderry, leased Killivittie, Knockenocher and Bellibughtbegg in the parish of Dumboe, County Londonderry, on 14 February 1656 from Lord Kirkcudbright. [PRONI.T640/59]

GYLLES, JOHN, mustered with sword and pike in the barony of Raphoe, County Donegal, 1630. [Donegal Muster Roll]

HADDOCK, JOHN, master of the Nightingale of Belfast trading to Glasgow in 1627. [CDG.2.587]

HAIRSCHAW, JOHN, absent from the town of Strathaven, probably a Covenanting refugee, to Ireland by 1683. [RPCS.VIII.653]

HALL, HUGH, in Magiligan, County Londonderry, 9 August 1666. [NAS.RH15.91.40]

HALL, JAMES, in the parish of Raphoe, County Donegal, 1665. [HTR]

HALL, JOHN, in Magiligan, County Londonderry, 9 August 1666. [NAS.RH15.91.40]

HAMILTON, Lady ALICE, wife of Sir Claude Hamilton of
Toome, County Antrim, petitioned King Charles I.
[CSPIre]

HAMILTON, ANDREW, in Dublin, 1720.
[NAS.GD10.1421.1.52]

HAMILTON, ARCHIBALD, 1659. [NAS.RH15.91.38]

HAMILTON, Sir CHARLES, of Castle Hamilton, Ireland,
1669. [NAS.AC7.4]

HAMILTON, CLAUD, Captain of the Earl of Lindsay's
Regiment at Carrickfergus in September 1642. [DS#334]

HAMILTON, FRANCIS, of Killiner, in the parish of Raphoe,
County Donegal, 1665. [HTR]

HAMILTON, Lieutenant GAVIN, a receipt, 1672.
[NAS.RH15.91.39]

HAMILTON, GEORGE, in Coleraine, County Londonderry,
1677. [PRONI.T640/129]

HAMILTON, HANS, 1659. [NAS.RH15.91.38]

HAMILTON, Sir HANS, was granted lands in County
Tipperary, County Waterford, County Roscommon,
County Kildare, County Kilkenny, and County Clare, on
19 February 1666. [CSPIre]

HAMILTON, Sir HANS, of Hamilton's Bawn, was granted
lands in County Tyrone on 12 January 1670. [CSPIre]

HAMILTON, HANS, a minor, 1682. [PRONI.T640/134]

HAMILTON, HELEN, a refugee from Ireland, 1689.
[NAS.CH2.635.1/65]

HAMILTON, HUGH, was granted the townland of Lisdivin
in the parish of Donagheady, County Tyrone, on 1
January 1615. [PRONI.D623/B13/2A]

HAMILTON, JAMES, of Kirktown, Scotland, leased land in County Tyrone and County Fermanagh, 22 August 1612. [PRONI.T640/3]

HAMILTON, Sir JAMES, in Bangor, County Down, was assigned leases of Balle-Lambegg, Balle-Dumkeagh, Tullnecrosse, Slutmeales, in County Down, in May 1622. [PRONI.T640/18]

HAMILTON, JAMES, was granted lands in County Tyrone on 12 January 1670. [CSPIre]

HAMILTON, JAMES, Marquis óf, was granted lands in County Down in 1636. [NNAS.NRAS.2177/bundle 3546]

HAMILTON, JOHN, mustered unarmed in the barony of Raphoe, County Donegal, 1630. [Donegal Muster Roll]

HAMILTON, JOHN, Captain of the Earl of Eglinton's Regiment in Bangor on 9 September 1642. [DS#333]

HAMILTON, JOHN, Lieutenant Colonel of the Earl of Lindsay's Regiment at Carrickfergus in September 1642. [DS#334]

HAMILTON, JOHN, a witness in Dungannon, County Tyrone, 8 March 1667. [CSPIre]

HAMILTON, JOHN, a tenant on William Conyngham's lands in County Londonderry, 1683. [DP/Lenox-Conyngham pp]

HAMILTON, ROBERT, Captain of the Earl of Lindsay's Regiment at Carrickfergus in September 1642. [DS#334]

HAMILTON, WILLIAM. Sasine of William Hamilton, merchant, and his wife now in Strabane, Ireland, and James Hamilton, burgess of Glasgow, their son, in the wester booth of the Market Cross of Linlithgow. 20 June 1620. [NAS.B48.18.140]

HAMILTON, WILLIAM, of Ballymorgan, County Down, 1622. [NAS.RH15.91.38]

HAMILTON, WILLIAM, of Ballymechan, County Down, 1622. [PRONI.T640/17]

HAMILTON, WILLIAM, Captain of the Campbell of Lawers Regiment at Temple Patrick on 10 September 1642. [DS#335]

HAMILTON, WILLIAM, of Lough Currin, County Tyrone, 12 February 1666. [CSPIre]

HAMILTON, WILLIAM, a witness in Dungannon, County Tyrone, 8 March 1667. [CSPIre]

HAMILTON, WILLIAM, of Caledon, was granted lands in County Tyrone on 12 January 1670. [CSPIre]

HAMILTON, WILLIAM, a tenant on William Conyngham's lands in County Londonderry, 1683. [DP/Lenox-Conyngham pp]

HAMILTON, ...,of Pristhill, parish of Blantyre, probably a Covenanting refugee, to Ireland by 1683. [RPCS.VIII.649]

HAMMELL, ALEXANDER, in Braidisland, County Antrim, 1613. [NAS.GD97.Sec.1/335]

HAMMOND, ALEXANDER, mustered unarmed in the barony of Raphoe, County Donegal, 1630. [Donegal Muster Roll]

HANNA, JOHN, in Carrickfergus, with wife Margaret Drummond, and children James, Margaret, and Robert, 1683. [NAS.RD2/61/299, 301, 303]

HANNAY, WILLIAM, a yeoman in Killowen, County Londonderry, leased Ballemore in the parish of Killowen, County Londonderry, 10 October 1631. [PRONI.T640/27]

HARPER, JOHN, mustered with sword in the barony of Raphoe, County Donegal, 1630. [Donegal Muster Roll]

HARRELL, HUGH, in Strabane, County Tyrone, in March 1688. [NAS.AC7.9]

HARRIS, JOHN, in the parish of Raphoe, County Donegal, 1665. [HTR]

HART, JOHN, a non-conformist minister who had been imprisoned for seven years in Lifford gaol, petitioned King Charles II for his release, 1669. [CSPIre]

HAY, JOHN, in Dublin, probate 1671 PCC

HAYES, NICHOLAS, a skipper in Dublin, 1717. [NAS.AC13.1.192; AC8.212]

HENDERSON, ARCHIBALD, mustered with a sword in the barony of Raphoe, County Donegal, 1630. [Donegal Muster Roll]

HENDERSON, DANIEL, in the parish of Raphoe, County Donegal, 1665. [HTR]

HENDERSON, GAVIN, in Hetlandhill, parish of Mouswald, a merchant who traded in Ireland, 1652. [Mouswald Kirk Session Records]

HENDERSON, HUGH, of Lissmontegly, in the parish of Raphoe, County Donegal, 1665. [HTR]

HENDERSON, JAMES, in the parish of Raphoe, County Donegal, 1665. [HTR]

HENDERSON, JAMES, a merchant from Glasgow, trading in Belfast in July 1685. [NAS.AC7.7]

HENDERSON, JOHN, mustered unarmed in the barony of Raphoe, County Donegal, 1630. [Donegal Muster Roll]

HENDERSON, JOHN, of Rusby, in the parish of Raphoe, County Donegal, 1665. [HTR]

HENDERSON, MICHAEL, mustered unarmed in the barony of Raphoe, County Donegal, 1630. [Donegal Muster Roll]

HENDERSON, MICHAEL, of Carrickbreak, in the parish of Raphoe, County Donegal, 1665. [HTR]

HENDERSON, QUINTIN, a tenant on William Conyngham's lands in County Londonderry, 1683. [DP/Lenox-Conyngham pp]

HENDERSON, RICHARD, in the barony of Magherasterhana and Clankeilly, County Fermanagh, 1631. [Fermanagh Muster Roll]

HENDERSON, ROBERT, in the parish of Raphoe, County Donegal, 1665. [HTR]

HENDERSON, SIMON, in the barony of Magherasterhana and Clankeilly, County Fermanagh, 1631. [Fermanagh Muster Roll]

HENDERSON, THOMAS, mustered unarmed in the barony of Raphoe, County Donegal, 1630. [Donegal Muster Roll]

HENDERSON, THOMAS, in the parish of Raphoe, County Donegal, 1665. [HTR]

HENDERSON, WILLIAM, in the parish of Raphoe, County Donegal, 1665. [HTR]

HENDRIE, MARGARET, from Irvine, Ayrshire, a resident of Coleraine, County Londonderry, wife of Quintin Mure, 1618. [AG.IV.30]

HENDRY, JAMES, in County Fermanagh, 1631. [Fermanagh Muster Roll]

HENRY, ANDREW, in Anlow, County Londonderry, 9
August 1666. [NAS.RH15.91.40]

HENRY, WALTER, mustered unarmed in the barony of
Raphoe, County Donegal, 1630. [Donegal Muster Roll]

HENRY, WILLIAM, mustered with a sword in the barony of
Raphoe, County Donegal, 1630. [Donegal Muster Roll]

HENRYSON, JANET, daughter of Hugh Henryson a weaver
burgess of Irvine, residing in Dundovan, County Antrim,
1618. [AG.IV.57]

HEPBURN, ROBERT, Captain of Home of the Heugh's
Regiment at Carrickfergus on 9 September 1642.
[DS#336]

HERIOT, ARCHIBALD, late of County Down, and his
widow Elizabeth Patillo, charter re property in Cupar,
Fife, 1667. [RGS.XI.1004]

HESLET, JOHN, mustered with a sword in the barony of
Raphoe, County Donegal, 1630. [Donegal Muster Roll]

HEWES, WILLIAM, mustered unarmed in the barony of
Raphoe, County Donegal, 1630. [Donegal Muster Roll]

HILL, JOHN, of Craigiehill, parish of Govan, probably a
Covenanting refugee, to Ireland by 1683.
[RPCS.VIII.645]

HISLAT, THOMAS, mustered with a sword and snaphance in
the barony of Raphoe, Donegal, 1630. [Donegal Muster
Roll]

HOBKIN, ALEXANDER, miller at Bushmills, Ireland,
husband of Janet Martin, daughter of John Martin a
burgess of Irvine, 1615, 1618. [AG.IV.151; VII.141]

HOGG, WILLIAM, and his wife Jane, 1682; versus Sir
Robert Maxwell and Ann, Countess of Clanbrazil, 21
June 1683. [NAS.RH15.91.40][PRONI.T640A/8]

HOLLIDAY, the widow, a tenant, May 1672.
[NAS.RH15.91.40]

HOME, JOHN, Major of the Earl of Leven's Regiment in
Carrickfergus, 9 September 1642. [DS#328]

HOME, ROBERT, Colonel of Home of the Heugh's
Regiment at Carrickfergus on 9 September 1642.
[DS#336]

HOME. ROBERT, Captain Colonel of the Lifeguard of Foot
at Donaghadee on 14 September 1642. [DS#339]

HOMES, GABRIEL, of Ardernock, in the parish of Raphoe,
County Donegal, 1665. [HTR]

HOMES, JAMES, in the parish of Raphoe, County Donegal,
1665. [HTR]

HOMES, JOHN, [1], in the parish of Raphoe, County
Donegal, 1665. [HTR]

HOMES, JOHN, [2], in the parish of Raphoe, County
Donegal, 1665. [HTR]

HOMMELL, MATTHEW, a merchant in Irvine, Ayrshire,
then in Dunluce, Ireland, husband of Bessie Tran, 15
December 1618. [NAS.RS11.1.265]

HOUSTON, ALEXANDER, second son of William Houston
of Cottreoche, and Annas Edmonstone, sister of William
Edmonstone of Braidisland, County Antrim, marriage
contract dated 10 September 1625. The said Alexander
Houston had leases of the lands of Drumkein,
Culladurrie and Lochnamanon from Andrew, Bishop of
Raphoe. [NAS.GD97.Sec.1/381]

HOUSTON, DAVID, [1633-1696], a Presbyterian minister in
Glenarm and Ballymoney. [NLS.Wod.Fol.XXVI/225,
4136]

HOUSTON, DAVID, receipt dated 1662. [NAS.RH15.91.40]

HOUSTON, FINLAY, mustered with a sword in the barony of Raphoe, County Donegal, 1630. [Donegal Muster Roll]

HOUSTON, JAMES, mustered with a sword in the barony of Raphoe, County Donegal, 1630. [Donegal Muster Roll]

HOUSTON, JOHN, in Dungiven, County Londonderry, 1630. [Dungiven Muster Roll]

HOUSTON, JOHN, Captain of the Earl of Glencairn's Regiment in Carrickfergus on 9 September 1642. [DS#331]

HOUSTON, Captain WILLIAM, a letter dated 1672. [NLS.Wod.Fol.XXVI.225]

HOWAT, EDWARD, mustered unarmed in the barony of Raphoe, County Donegal, 1630. [Donegal Muster Roll]

HUCHEON, JOHN, mustered unarmed in the barony of Raphoe, County Donegal, 1630. [Donegal Muster Roll]

HUGH, WILLIAM, in the parish of Raphoe, County Donegal, 1665. [HTR]

HUGHES, DAVID, in the parish of Raphoe, County Donegal, 1665. [HTR]

HUME, ALEXANDER, in the barony of Magheraboy, County Fermanagh, 1631. [Fermanagh Muster Roll]

HUME, DAVID, mustered with sword and snaphance in the barony of Raphoe, County Donegal, 1630. [Donegal Muster Roll]

HUME, PATRICK, in the barony of Magheraboy, County Fermanagh, 1631. [Fermanagh Muster Roll]

HUNTER, ARCHIBALD, mustered unarmed in the barony of Raphoe, County Donegal, 1630. [Donegal Muster Roll]

HUNTER, HENRY, in barony of Raphoe, 1630. [Donegal Muster Roll]

HUNTER, JOHN, (1), in barony of Raphoe, 1630. [Donegal Muster Roll]

HUNTER, JOHN, (2), in barony of Raphoe, 1630. [Donegal Muster Roll]

HUNTER, J., in the parish of Raphoe, County Donegal, 1665. [HTR]

HUNTER, PATRICK, of Hunterston, to Ireland in November 1673. [HH.83]

HUTCHESON, ARCHIBALD, in the Routt or the Glens of Antrim, a witness in 1661. [CSP.Ire.1661]

HUTCHISON, JAMES, mustered with sword and pike in the barony of Raphoe, County Donegal, 1630. [Donegal Muster Roll]

HUTTON, THOMAS, mustered unarmed in the barony of Raphoe, County Donegal, 1630. [Donegal Muster Roll]

HYNDMAN, DAVID, a receipt dated 1662. [NAS.RH15.91.40]

HYNDMAN, HECTOR, mustered with a sword in the barony of Raphoe, County Donegal, 1630. [Donegal Muster Roll]

HYNDMAN, ROBERT, a tenant in Ardillan, 1663. [NAS.RH15.91.38C]

HYNEMAN, JOHN, in the parish of Raphoe, County Donegal, 1665. [HTR]

INNES, WILLIAM, Captain of Lord Sinclair's Regiment in Newry on 28 September 1642. [DS#337]

IRVINE, GERALD, an assizeman in Dungannon, County Tyrone, 8 March 1667. [CSPIre]

IRVING, CHARLES, of Castle Irving, County Fermanagh, 1721. [NAS.AC8.260]

IRVING, GEORGE, mustered with a sword and pike in the barony of Raphoe, County Donegal, 1630. [Donegal Muster Roll]

IRVING, JOHN, 1695. [NAS.RH15.91.39]

IRWIN, ANDREW, in the barony of Magherasterhana and Clankeilly, County Fermanagh, 1631. [Fermanagh Muster Roll]

IRWIN, DAVID, in the barony of Magherasterhana and Clankeilly, County Fermanagh, 1631. [Fermanagh Muster Roll]

IRWIN, GEORGE, in the barony of Magheraboy, County Fermanagh, 1631. [Fermanagh Muster Roll]

IRWIN, JOHN, in the barony of Magherasterhana and Clankeilly, County Fermanagh, 1631. [Fermanagh Muster Roll]

IRWIN, JOHN, in the barony of Magheraboy, County Fermanagh, 1631. [Fermanagh Muster Roll]

JACKSON, JAMES, receipt dated 1662. [NAS.RH15.91.40]

JOHNSON, JOHN, in the parish of Raphoe, County Donegal, 1665. [HTR]

JOHNSTON, ADAM, in the barony of Magheraboy, County Fermanagh, 1631. [Fermanagh Muster Roll]

JOHNSTON, ADAM, in Bellyeares, County Armagh, bond with Thomas Lewars a merchant burgess of Dumfries, dated 22 August 1672, registered 1673. [Dumfries Commissary minute book]

JOHNSTON, ALEXANDER, mustered with a sword in the barony of Raphoe, County Donegal, 1630. [Donegal Muster Roll]

JOHNSTON, ANDREW, in the barony of Magheraboy, County Fermanagh, 1631. [Fermanagh Muster Roll]

JOHNSTON, ARTHUR, in the barony of Magherasterhana and Clankeilly, County Fermanagh, 1631. [Fermanagh Muster Roll]

JOHNSTON, ARTHUR, in the barony of Magheraboy, County Fermanagh, 1631. [Fermanagh Muster Roll]

JOHNSTON, DAVID, in the barony of Magheraboy, County Fermanagh, 1631. [Fermanagh Muster Roll]

JOHNSTON, FRANCIS, in the barony of Magherasterhana and Clankeilly, County Fermanagh, 1631. [Fermanagh Muster Roll]

JOHNSTON, FRANCIS, in the barony of Magheraboy, County Fermanagh, 1631. [Fermanagh Muster Roll]

JOHNSTON, HENRY, in the barony of Magheraboy, County Fermanagh, 1631. [Fermanagh Muster Roll]

JOHNSTON, JAMES, mustered with a sword and pike in the barony of Raphoe, County Donegal, 1630. [Donegal Muster Roll]

JOHNSTON, JAMES, in the barony of Magheraboy, County Fermanagh, 1631. [Fermanagh Muster Roll]

JOHNSTON, JAMES, in the barony of Magherasterhana and Clankeilly, County Fermanagh, 1631. [Fermanagh Muster Roll]

JOHNSTON, JAMES, in the parish of Raphoe, County Donegal, 1665. [HTR]

JOHNSTON, JOHN, in the barony of Magherasterhana and Clankeilly, County Fermanagh, 1631. [Fermanagh Muster Roll]

JOHNSTON, JOHN, in the barony of Magheraboy, County Fermanagh, 1631. [Fermanagh Muster Roll]

JOHNSTON, JOHN, a tenant of William Conyngham in Armagh, 1683. [DP/Lenox-Conyngham pp]

JOHNSTON, PATRICK, a merchant in Dublin, owner of the Martin of Dublin, then in Holyrood Abbey, 1715. [NAS.AC8.185; AC9.558; AC13.1.151]

JOHNSTON, RICHARD, in the barony of Magheraboy, County Fermanagh, 1631. [Fermanagh Muster Roll]

JOHNSTON, ROBERT, mustered unarmed in the barony of Raphoe, County Donegal, 1630. [Donegal Muster Roll]

JOHNSTON, ROBERT, in the barony of Magheraboy, County Fermanagh, 1631. [Fermanagh Muster Roll]

JOHNSTON, THOMAS, in the barony of Magheraboy, County Fermanagh, 1631. [Fermanagh Muster Roll]

JOHNSTON, WILLIAM, in the barony of Magheraboy, County Fermanagh, 1631. [Fermanagh Muster Roll]

JOHNSTON, WILLIAM, leased the lands called Calbrim McSparran, County Londonderry, from William Conyngham, 29 March 1695. [DP/Lenox-Conyngham pp]

KEIR, JAMES, mustered with a sword and pike in the barony of Raphoe, County Donegal, 1630. [Donegal Muster Roll]

KEIR, JOHN, master of the Speedwell from Londonderry to Bordeaux in 1655, captured and sold at Brest. [CSPIre.1657]

KEITH, J., 1659. [NAS.RH15.77.10]

KELSO, GAVIN, in Holywood, Ireland, leased land near Coleraine on 1 August 1617. [PRONI.T640/14]

KELSO, HUGH, a yeoman, and his wife in Gallanagh, parish of Urney, County Tyrone, 1660. [Poll Tax Returns]

KELSO, JAMES, mustered with a sword and a pike in the barony of Raphoe, County Donegal, 1630. [Donegal Muster Roll]

KELSO, JOHN, a servant in Gallanagh, parish of Urney, County Tyrone, 1660. [Poll Tax Returns]

KELSO, JOHN, from Ireland, a mariner aboard HMS Reformation, probate 1692 PCC

KELSO, THOMAS, mustered with a sword in the barony of Raphoe, County Donegal, 1630. [Donegal Muster Roll]

KENNEDY, DAVID, mustered in the barony of Raphoe, County Donegal, 1630. [Donegal Muster Roll]

KENNEDY, DAVID, in Newton, Ireland, 1645. [NLS.Wod.Fol.XXV/52]

KENNEDY, DAVID, a gentleman in Bangor, County Down, 22 May 1671. [PRONI.T640/113]

KENNEDY, JAMES, a messenger formerly in Maybole, Ayrshire, then in Bellicastle, Ireland, 20 September 1622. [NAS.RS11.2.395]

KENNEDY, JAMES, of the family of Ballymagowan, gentleman, born 1654, died 14 November 1726. [Clogher Cathedral gravestone]

KENNEDY, JOHN, mustered with a sword in the barony of Raphoe, County Donegal, 1630. [Donegal Muster Roll]

KENNEDY, Cornet JOHN, born 1617, died 17 July 1682. [Clogher Cathedral gravestone]

KENNEDY, JOHN, in Dublin, assigned leases to various lands in County Down, 1622. [NAS.RH15.91.38][PRONI.T640/17]

KENNEDY, ROBERT, in County Londonderry, 1632.
[NAS.RH15.91.32]

KENNEDY, ROBERT, Captain of Home of the Heugh's
Regiment at Carrickfergus on 9 September 1642.
[DS#336]

KENNEDY, ROBERT, in the Routt or the Glens of Antrim, a
witness in 1661. [CSP.Ire.1661]

KENNEDY, SILVESTER, a member of the House of
Commons in Ireland and one of "His Majesty's
distressed subjects of the Kingdom of Ireland", 1642.
[NA.SP.28/193]

KENNEDY, THOMAS, in Achbowie, County Antrim, and his
wife Janet Sinclair, daughter of David Sinclair in Barlae,
parish of Dalry, Scotland, 1628. [NAS.GD77.145]

KENNEDY, THOMAS, of Newtoun, 14 October 1674; 1675;
7 September 1675.
[NAS.RH15.91.40][PRONI.T640/125/127]

KERNE, THOMAS, son of John Kerne in Scotland, was
baptised on 11 November 1669 in Blaris, Lisburn,
County Down. [Blaris Parish Register]

KERR, DANIEL, in the parish of Raphoe, County Donegal,
1665. [HTR]

KERR, ELIZABETH, a refugee from Limerick, 1689.
[NAS.CH2.635.1/59]

KERR, JAMES, in the parish of Raphoe, County Donegal,
1665. [HTR]

KERR, JAMES, tenant in Riquaham, Ireland, 1721.
[NAS.GD97.1/649]

KERR, JOHN, minister at Monaghan, 1658. [CSA]

KERR, WILLIAM, Captain of the Earl of Lothian's Regiment
in Carrickfergus on 9 September 1642. [DS#329]

KETTLEWELL, WILLIAM, a merchant in Drogheda, 1722.
[LI#404]

KEY, JOHN, mustered with a sword in the barony of Raphoe,
County Donegal, 1630. [Donegal Muster Roll]

KIDD, HUGH, a merchant in Dunluce, County Antrim, 1687.
[NAS.GD201.2.3]

KIDD, WALTER, son of .....Kidd, now in Ireland, 1615.
[AG.VII.139]

KIL, WILLIAM, an assizeman in Dungannon, County
Tyrone, 8 March 1667. [CSPIre]

KILPATRICK, JOHN, mustered with a sword in the barony
of Raphoe, County Donegal, 1630. [Donegal Muster
Roll]

KILPATRICK, JOHN, in the barony of Magheraboy, County
Fermanagh, 1631. [Fermanagh Muster Roll]

KILPATRICK, JOHN, witness, 26 August 1656.
[NAS.RH15.91.38]

KINCAID, ALEXANDER, witness, 26 August 1656.
[NAS.RH15.91.38]

KINCAID, ANDREW, born 1678, son of Robert Kincaid and
his wife Agnes Donaldson, died 18 May 1725.
[Ballykeel, Islandmagee, gravestone]

KINCAID, Captain JOHN, born 1662, died in January 1730.
[Ballykeel, Islandmagee, gravestone]

KINCAID, ROBERT, born 1631, husband of Agnes
Donaldson, and father of Andrew Kincaid, died 22
January 1697. [Ballykeel, Islandmagee, gravestone]

KINGHORN, WILLIAM, mustered with a sword in the
barony of Raphoe, County Donegal, 1630. [Donegal
Muster Roll]

KIRKPATRICK, HERBERT, witness in Ardingall, County Donegal, 1628. [NAS.RH15.91.38]

KIRKPATRICK, JOHN, the elder, mustered with a sword in the barony of Raphoe, County Donegal, 1630. [Donegal Muster Roll]

KIRKPATRICK, JOHN, mustered unarmed in the barony of Raphoe, County Donegal, 1630. [Donegal Muster Roll]

KIRKWOOD, JAMES, in the parish of Raphoe, County Donegal, 1665. [HTR]

KNOX, ANDREW, mustered unarmed in the barony of Raphoe, County Donegal, 1630. [Donegal Muster Roll]

KNOX, GEORGE, a gentleman in Dunboe, County Londonderry, was granted a lease of Castle Toodrie, County Londonderry, on 20 April 1624 by Sir Robert McLelland. [PRONI.T640/21]

KNOX, GEORGE, mustered unarmed in the barony of Raphoe, County Donegal, 1630. [Donegal Muster Roll]

KNOX, JAMES, (1), mustered with sword and pike in the barony of Raphoe, County Donegal, 1630. [Donegal Muster Roll]

KNOX, JAMES, (2), in barony of Raphoe, 1630. [Donegal Muster Roll]

KNOX, JOHN, in the parish of Kilwaghter, 1652. [NAS.GD154.514]

KNOX, PATRICK, mustered unarmed in the barony of Raphoe, County Donegal, 1630. [Donegal Muster Roll]

KNOX, THOMAS, in the parish of Raphoe, County Donegal, 1665. [HTR]

KNOX, THOMAS, a merchant in Belfast, 1691. [NAS.RD3.LXXII.833-836]

KNOX, UCHTER, formerly of Ballyduffie, County Longford, a Royalist soldier who was wounded at the Battle of Dunbar in 1650. [CSPIre, 1660]

KNOX, WILLIAM, Captain of the Earl of Glencairn's Regiment in Carrickfergus on 9 September 1642. [DS#332]

KNOX, ..., late of Ballyduffie, County Longford, a Lieuteant of His Majesty's Life Guards, was killed at the Battle of Worcester in 1651. [CSPIre, 1660]

KYLE, ARCHIBALD, in the parish of Raphoe, County Donegal, 1665. [HTR]

KYLE, ROBERT, a merchant burgess of Irvine, residing at Gilligrun's Port, Ireland, 10 January 1617. [AG.VII.111]

LAIRD, ALEXANDER, [1], in the parish of Raphoe, County Donegal, 1665. [HTR]

LAIRD, ALEXANDER, [2], in the parish of Raphoe, County Donegal, 1665. [HTR]

LAIRD, JAMES, mustered with a sword in the barony of Raphoe, County Donegal, 1630. [Donegal Muster Roll]

LAIRD, JAMES, in the parish of Raphoe, County Donegal, 1665. [HTR]

LAIRD, JOHN, mustered with a sword in the barony of Raphoe, County Donegal, 1630. [Donegal Muster Roll]

LAIRD, JOHN, of Tulliveny, in the parish of Raphoe, County Donegal, 1665. [HTR]

LAIRD, ROBERT, of Assmoyne, in the parish of Raphoe, County Donegal, 1665. [HTR]

LAMBIE, MARGARET, spouse of James White in Bellistone, Ireland, sometime portioner of Whorleford, 7 January 1631. [NAS.RS11.5.2]

LANG, JOHN, mustered with sword and pike in the barony of
Raphoe, County Donegal, 1630. [Donegal Muster Roll]

LANG, WALTER, mustered unarmed in the barony of
Raphoe, County Donegal, 1630. [Donegal Muster Roll]

LARGS, ROBERT, mustered with a sword and musket in the
barony of Raphoe, County Donegal, 1630. [Donegal
Muster Roll]

LASSELLS, FRANCIS, mustered unarmed in the barony of
Raphoe, County Donegal, 1630. [Donegal Muster Roll]

LASSELLS, THOMAS, mustered with a snaphance in the
barony of Raphoe, County Donegal, 1630. [Donegal
Muster Roll]

LASSELLS, THOMAS, mustered unarmed in the barony of
Raphoe, County Donegal, 1630. [Donegal Muster Roll]

LASSELLS, WILLIAM, mustered unarmed in the barony of
Raphoe, County Donegal, 1630. [Donegal Muster Roll]

LAUGHLAN, WILLIAM, mustered with a sword in the
barony of Raphoe, County Donegal, 1630. [Donegal
Muster Roll]

LAUSON, JAMES, heirs, absent from the town of Strathaven,
probably a Covenanting refugee, to Ireland by 1683.
[RPCS.VIII.653]

LAW, WILLIAM, a yeoman, with his wife, in Gallanagh,
parish of Urney, County Tyrone, 1660. [Poll Tax
Returns]

LAWRY, ANDREW, in the parish of Raphoe, County
Donegal, 1665. [HTR]

LAWRY, PATRICK, in the parish of Raphoe, County
Donegal, 1665. [HTR]

LAWSON, ALEXANDER, mustered with a sword in the barony of Raphoe, Donegal, 1630. [Donegal Muster Roll]

LEAY, HUGH, mustered with sword and pike in the barony of Raphoe, County Donegal, 1630. [Donegal Muster Roll]

LECKY, ANDREW, mustered with a sword in the barony of Raphoe, County Donegal, 1630. [Donegal Muster Roll]

LECKY, ROBERT, mustered with a sword in the barony of Raphoe, County Donegal, 1630. [Donegal Muster Roll]

LEECH, ALEXANDER, in the parish of Kilwaghter, 1652. [NAS.GD154.514]

LEECH, JAMES, mustered with sword and snaphance in the barony of Raphoe, County Donegal, 1630. [Donegal Muster Roll]

LEECH, PATRICK. mustered with sword in the barony of Raphoe, County Donegal, 1630. [Donegal Muster Roll]

LEIPER, ANDREW, mustered with a sword in the barony of Raphoe, County Donegal, 1630. [Donegal Muster Roll]

LEITCH, JOHN, mustered unarmed in the barony of Raphoe, County Donegal, 1630. [Donegal Muster Roll]

LEITHES, WILLIAM, in Newton, Ireland, 1645. [NLS.Wod.Fol.XXV/52]

LEMON, ROBERT, mustered unarmed in the barony of Raphoe, County Donegal, 1630. [Donegal Muster Roll]

LENNOX, DANIEL, in the barony of Magherasterhana and Clankeilly, County Fermanagh, 1631. [Fermanagh Muster Roll]

LENNOX, DONALD, in County Fermanagh, 1631. [Fermanagh Muster Roll]

LENNOX, JAMES, mustered with a sword in the barony of Raphoe, Donegal, 1630. [Donegal Muster Roll]

LENNOX, JAMES, Captain of the Campbell of Lawers Regiment at Temple Patrick on 10 September 1642. [DS#335]

LESLEY, JOHN, a merchant in Coleraine, 1710. [NAS.AC10.100]

LESLIE, ANDREW, Captain of Major General Robert Monro's Regiment in Carrickfergus on 9 September 1642. [DS#329]

LESLIE, JAMES, in the parish of Raphoe, County Donegal, 1665. [HTR]

LESLIE, JOHN, Captain of the Earl of Leven's Regiment in Carrickfergus, 9 September 1642. [DS#328]

LESLIE, JOHN, Captain of Major General Robert Monro's Regiment in Carrickfergus on 9 September 1642. [DS#329]

LESLIE, PATRICK or PETER, General Adjutant of Lord Sinclair's Regiment in Newry on 28 September 1642. [DS#337]

LESLIE, WILLIAM, and **JANET GORDON** his wife, refugees from County Antrim, 1689. [NAS.CH2.635.1/60]

LEWERS, MATHEW, butcher in Newton, County Down, 1640. [HH.80]

LIDDERDAIL, JAMES, 1627. [NAS.RH15.91.39]

LIDDERDAIL, JAMES, Captain of Major General Robert Monro's Regiment in Carrickfergus on 9 September 1642. [DS#329]

LINDSAY, ANDREW, Captain of the Earl of Lothian's Regiment in Carrickfergus on 9 September 1642. [DS#329]

LINDSAY, DAVID, in the parish of Raphoe, County Donegal, 1665. [HTR]

LINDSAY, JOHN, mustered with a sword and pike in the barony of Raphoe, County Donegal, 1630. [Donegal Muster Roll]

LINDSAY, JOHN, of Naghrythan, in the parish of Raphoe, County Donegal, 1665. [HTR]

LINDSAY, MATTHEW, mustered with a sword in the barony of Raphoe, County Donegal, 1630. [Donegal Muster Roll]

LINDSAY, MICHAEL, mustered with a sword in the barony of Raphoe, County Donegal, 1630. [Donegal Muster Roll]

LINDSAY, ROBERT, mustered with a sword in the barony of Raphoe, County Donegal, 1630. [Donegal Muster Roll]

LINDSAY, WILLIAM, mustered with a sword and snaphance in the barony of Raphoe, County Donegal, 1630. [Donegal Muster Roll]

LITTLE, ANDREW, in the barony of Magherstefeny (?), County Fermanagh, 1631. [Fermanagh Muster Roll]

LITTLE, JAMES, in the barony of Magherasterhana and Clankeilly, County Fermanagh, 1631. [Fermanagh Muster Roll]

LITTLE, JOHN, in the barony of Magherasterhana and Clankeilly, County Fermanagh, 1631. [Fermanagh Muster Roll]

LITTLE, THOMAS, in the barony of Magherstefeny (?), County Fermanagh, 1631. [Fermanagh Muster Roll]

LITTLE, THOMAS, in the barony of Magheraboy, County Fermanagh, 1631. [Fermanagh Muster Roll]

LITTLE, WALTER, in the barony of Magherasterhana and Clankeilly, County Fermanagh, 1631. [Fermanagh Muster Roll]

LITTLE, WILLIAM, in County Fermanagh, 1631. [Fermanagh Muster Roll]

LITTLE, WILLIAM, in the barony of Magherasterhana and Clankeilly, County Fermanagh, 1631. [Fermanagh Muster Roll]

LIVINGSTONE, JAMES, of Kyle, 1633. [NAS.RH15.91.39]

LIVINGSTONE, MARY, in Donaghadee, County Down, a letter dated 7 November 1672. [PRONI.T640/118]

LIVISTON, ARCHIBALD, mustered with a sword and snaphance in the barony of Raphoe, County Donegal, 1630. [Donegal Muster Roll]

LOCKHART, HUGH, mustered with sword in the barony of Raphoe, County Donegal, 1630. [Donegal Muster Roll]

LOCKHART, Sir JAMES, Captain of the Earl of Lothian's Regiment in Carrickfergus on 9 September 1642. [DS#329]

LOCKHART, THOMAS, in the barony of Magheraboy, County Fermanagh, 1631. [Fermanagh Muster Roll]

LOGAN, JAMES, mustered unarmed in the barony of Raphoe, County Donegal, 1630. [Donegal Muster Roll]

LOGAN, ROBERT, in Broadisland, Ireland, was served heir to his late uncle Walter Logan there, on 10 July 1669. [NAS.GD97.Sec.1/511]

LONG, WALTER, receipt dated 1662. [NAS.RH15.91.40]

LONGE,......, in the parish of Raphoe, County Donegal, 1665. [HTR]

LOVE, JOHN, a merchant in Londonderry, 1720. [NAS.AC9.675]

LOWRIE, JOHN, mustered with a sword in the barony of Raphoe, County Donegal, 1630. [Donegal Muster Roll]

LOWRIE, THOMAS, mustered with a sword in the barony of Raphoe, County Donegal, 1630. [Donegal Muster Roll]

LOWRIE, WALTER, mustered unarmed in the barony of Raphoe, County Donegal, 1630. [Donegal Muster Roll]

LYN, WILLIAM, in the parish of Raphoe, County Donegal, son and heir of the late Margaret Muir, a disposition in favour of Thomas Reid in Auchindowy, County Londonderry, 23 November 1665. [NAS.GD1.693.13]

LYNE, WILLIAM, mustered with a sword in the barony of Raphoe, County Donegal, 1630. [Donegal Muster Roll]

LYON, DUNCAN, mustered with sword and pike in the barony of Raphoe, County Donegal, 1630. [Donegal Muster Roll]

LYON, JOHN, mustered with sword and pike in the barony of Raphoe, County Donegal, 1630. [Donegal Muster Roll]

LYON, JOHN, mustered unarmed in the barony of Raphoe, County Donegal, 1630. [Donegal Muster Roll]

LYON, ROBERT, mustered with a sword and snaphance in the barony of Raphoe, County Donegal, 1630. [Donegal Muster Roll]

LYON, WILLIAM, mustered with a sword and snaphance in the barony of Raphoe, County Donegal, 1630. [Donegal Muster Roll]

MCADOWE, JAMES, mustered with a sword and snaphance in the barony of Raphoe, County Donegal, 1630. [Donegal Muster Roll]

MCALEXANDER, GEORGE, of Ballygrooby, a yeoman in County Londonderry, 1696. [DP]

MCALEXANDER, THOMAS, provost of Strabane, County Tyrone, 21 December 1631. [NAS.E661.142]

MCANDREW, THOMAS, a laborer in Gallanagh, parish of Urney, County Tyrone, 1660. [Poll Tax Returns]

MACARTHUR, ARTHUR, mustered with curasses and gorget in the barony of Raphoe, County Donegal, 1630. [Donegal Muster Roll]

MCARTHUR, ROBERT, in Magiligan, County Londonderry, 9 August 1666. [NAS.RH15.91.40]

MCARTHUR, THOMAS, mustered with a sword in the barony of Raphoe, County Donegal, 1630. [Donegal Muster Roll]

MACAULAY, ALEXANDER, Captain of the Marquis of Argyll's Regiment at Ballycastle on 17 November 1642. [DS#338]

MCAULAY, ALEXANDER, in the Routt or the Glens of Antrim, a witness in 1661. [CSP.Ire.1661]

MCAULAY, JOHN, mustered with a sword in the barony of Raphoe, County Donegal, 1630. [Donegal Muster Roll]

MCBRAIR, ROBERT, 7 February 1695. [NAS.RH15.91.39]

MCBURNIE, WILLIAM, mustered unarmed in the barony of Raphoe, County Donegal, 1630. [Donegal Muster Roll]

MCCAIRTY, ..., an Irish pirate who was active off the coast of Kirkcudbrightshire in 1698, was captured and imprisoned in Stranraer Tolbooth in 1699. [NAS.GD248.594.6]

MCCALLA, ARCHIBALD, mustered with a sword in the barony of Raphoe, County Donegal, 1630. [Donegal Muster Roll]

MCCALLA, JOHN, mustered with a sword in the barony of Raphoe, County Donegal, 1630. [Donegal Muster Roll]

MCCARTNEY, GEORGE, a merchant in Belfast, 11 November 1674, 31 March 1675, 4 January 1676. [PRONI.T640/123/125] [NAS.RH15.91.40]

MCCARTNEY, GEORGE, in Belfast, County Antrim, probate 1694 PCC

MCCARTNEY, ISAAC, a merchant in Belfast, 1722. [NAS.AC9.849]

MCCARTNEY, JOHN, mustered in the barony of Raphoe, County Donegal, 1630. [Donegal Muster Roll]

MCCAYLEY, WILLIAM, in the parish of Kilwaghter, 1652. [NAS.GD154.514]

MACHAN, WILLIAM, mustered with sword in the barony of Raphoe, County Donegal, 1630. [Donegal Muster Roll]

MCCHENEY, ANDREW, mustered unarmed in the barony of Raphoe, County Donegal, 1630. [Donegal Muster Roll]

MCCHENEY, JOHN, mustered unarmed in the barony of Raphoe, County Donegal, 1630. [Donegal Muster Roll]

MCCLEAN, DAVID, born 1661, late of Kilnahushogue, died 8 February 1714. [Clogher Cathedral gravestone]

MACLEAN, JOHN, from Belfast, a mariner on the Warrington at Guinea, probate 1692 PCC

MCCLEARY, JAMES, in the parish of Raphoe, County Donegal, 1665. [HTR]

MCCLEARY, MICHAEL, mustered unarmed in the barony of Raphoe, County Donegal, 1630. [Donegal Muster Roll]

MCCLELLAN, EDWARD, a gentleman in the parish of Dunboe, County Londonderry, leased Ringrashbegg, County Londonderry, on 24 July 1655. [PRONI.T640/69]

MCCLELLAN, JOHN, a gentleman, leased Donallies in the parish of Dunboe, County Londonderry, 5 August 1655. [PRONI.T640/70]

MCCLELLAN, ROBERT, of Killiboag, 1722. [NAS.NRAS#231, bundle 13/447]

MCCLELLAN, WILLIAM, of Drumbegge, Ireland, was appointed as an attorney for the lands of Balliboe in Bradelin, County Londonderry, and of Enish Conohor, Balle Quege, County Londonderry, 29 April 1617. [PRONI.T640/9/10]

MCCLELLAN, WILLIAM, Captain of the Earl of Leven's Regiment in Carrickfergus, 9 September 1642. [DS#328]

MCCLELLAN, WILLIAM, of Bally..., a witness, 26 August 1656. [NAS.RH15.91.38]

MCCLELLAND, EDWARD, a receipt dated 1662. [NAS.RH15.91.40]

MCCLELLAND, GILBERT, in Gray Abbey, County Down, 1610. [Laing#1582]

MCCLELLAND, JAMES, of Auchenhay, in Gray Abbey, County Down, 1610. [Laing#1582]

MCCLELLAND, JOHN, of Barbie (?), a freeholder in Ulster, 1620s. [NAS.RH15.91.33]

MCCLELLAND, JOHN, of Orchardton, a freeholder in Ulster, 1620s. [NAS.RH15.91.33]

MCCLELLAND, JOHN, in Anlow, County Londonderry, 9 August 1666. [NAS.RH15.91.40]

MCCLELLAND, JOHN, a vagabond from Ireland who settled in the parish of Urr, Dumfries-shire, by 1684. [RPCS.IX.398]

MCCLELLAND, MARY, 29 May 1623. [PRONI.T640/22]

MCCLELLAND, PATRICK, mustered with a sword and snaphance in the barony of Raphoe, Donegal, 1630. [Donegal Muster Roll]

MCCLELLAND, ROBERT, of Bombie, a freeholder in Ulster, 1620s. [NAS.RH15.91.33]

MCCLELLAND, Sir ROBERT, in Ballycastle, County Londonderry, 1624, 1628, 1631, 1632. [NAS.RH15.91.32/38] [PRONI.T640/24; 640A/13]

MCCLELLAND, ROBERT, in Ardkillin, County Londonderry, lease, 1 June 1634. [PRONI.T640/35]

MCCLELLAND, THOMAS, in Gray Abbey, County Down, 1610. [Laing#1582]

MCCLELLAND, THOMAS, a gentleman in the parish of Dunboe, County Londonderry, leased Belliehacket Clanihony, Dunboe, on 13 August 1655. [PRONI.T640/74][NAS.RH15.91.40]

MCCLELLAND, WILLIAM, of Orchardton, a freeholder in Ulster, 1620s. [NAS.RH15.91.33]

MCCLELLAND, WILLIAM, of Mallork, (?), a freeholder in Ulster, 1620s. [NAS.RH15.91.33]

MCCLELLANE, or MCKLEANE, ..., Captain of the Marquis of Argyll's Regiment at Ballymoney on 18 November 1642. [DS#338]

MCCLENNYE, JAMES, a servant in Gallanagh, parish of Urney, County Tyrone, 1660. [Poll Tax Returns]

MCCLERE, JOHN, mustered with a sword in the barony of Raphoe, County Donegal, 1630. [Donegal Muster Roll]

MCCLINTOCK, ALEXANDER, mustered with a sword and a pike in the barony of Raphoe, County Donegal, 1630. [Donegal Muster Roll]

MCCLINTOCK, FINLAY, mustered with a sword in the barony of Raphoe, County Donegal, 1630. [Donegal Muster Roll]

MCCLINTOCK, JAMES, in the parish of Raphoe, County Donegal, 1665. [HTR]

MCCLINTOCK, JOHN, mustered unarmed in the barony of Raphoe, County Donegal, 1630. [Donegal Muster Roll]

MCCLINTOCK, JOHN, of Maghoihee, in the parish of Raphoe, County Donegal, 1665. [HTR]

MCCLINTOCK, ROBERT, in the parish of Raphoe, County Donegal, 1665. [HTR]

MACLORE, ANDREW, a mariner from Holywood, Ireland, who died aboard HMS Southampton, probate 1696 PCC

MCCLURE, JOHN, of Agagalty, in the parish of Raphoe, County Donegal, 1665. [HTR]

MCCLURE, ROBERT, in the parish of Raphoe, County Donegal, 1665. [HTR]

MCCOLLUM, HUGH, a merchant in Dunluce, County Antrim, 1687. [NAS.GD201.2.3]

MCCOLM, WILLIAM, in the parish of Auchlan or Achlow(?), County Londonderry, an indenture or lease with Robert Maxwell of Orchardton, 29 October 1646, [NAS.RH15.91.32][PRONI.T640/55]

MCCOMBE, JOHN, of Achalow(?), aged 40, witness, 26 August 1656. [NAS.RH15.91.38]

MCCOMBE, JOHN, a receipt dated 1662. [NAS.RH15.91.40]

MCCOMBE, THOMAS, in Anlow, County Londonderry, 9 August 1666. [NAS.RH15.91.40]

MCCOMBIE, JAMES, Captain of the Earl of Eglinton's Regiment in Bangor on 9 September 1642. [DS#333]

MCCONNELL, DONNELL, mustered unarmed in the barony of Raphoe, County Donegal, 1630. [Donegal Muster Roll]

MCCONNELL, GAVIN, mustered unarmed in the barony of Raphoe, County Donegal, 1630. [Donegal Muster Roll]

MACCONNELL, JOHN, of Brocsinemart, leased lands in Glencorme from Archibald Edmonstone of Braidisland, 15 July 1627. [NAS.GD97.Sec.1/388]

MCCONNELL, MORRIS, mustered with a sword and a pike in the barony of Raphoe, County Donegal, 1630. [Donegal Muster Roll]

MCCONOCHY, JOHN, mustered with a sword in the barony of Raphoe, County Donegal, 1630. [Donegal Muster Roll]

MCCORKILL, ANDREW, mustered with sword and pike in barony of Raphoe, County Donegal, 1630. [Donegal Muster Roll]

MCCORKILL, JOHN, mustered with sword and pike in the barony of Raphoe, County Donegal,1630. [Donegal Muster Roll]

MCCORMICK, JOHN, in the parish of Raphoe, County Donegal, 1665. [HTR]

MCCORNOK, JOHN, son of John McCornok in Ireland and his wife Christian Sym, 10 April 1628. [NAS.RS11.4.223]

MCCOSHINE, DUNCAN, mustered with sword and pike in the barony of Raphoe, County Donegal, 1630. [Donegal Muster Roll]

MCCREARY, JAMES, mustered with a sword in the barony of Raphoe, County Donegal, 1630. [Donegal Muster Roll]

MCCREARY, JOHN, mustered with a sword in the barony of Raphoe, County Donegal, 1630. [Donegal Muster Roll]

MCCREAY, JAMES, mustered with a sword and snaphance in the barony of Raphoe, Donegal, 1630. [Donegal Muster Roll]

MCCREDY, FINLAY, mustered with sword in the barony of Raphoe, County Donegal, 1630. [Donegal Muster Roll]

MCCUBIN, PATRICK, a receipt dated 1662. [NAS.RH15.91.40]

MCCULLOCH, ALEXANDER, from Ballycopeland, County Down, emigrated to America in 1718. [NAS.GD10.1421]

MCCULLOCH, Captain JAMES, a merchant in Belfast, owner of the <u>Mary of Belfast</u>, bound for Barbados, 1726. [NAS.AC9.967]

MCCULLOGH, JOHN, mustered in the barony of Raphoe, County Donegal, 1630. [Donegal Muster Roll]

MCCULVER, ALEXANDER, mustered unarmed in the barony of Raphoe, County Donegal, 1630. [Donegal Muster Roll]

MCCULVER, RICHARD, mustered unarmed in the barony of Raphoe, County Donegal, 1630. [Donegal Muster Roll]

MCCURRIN, ARTHUR, mustered with sword in the barony of Raphoe, County Donegal, 1630. [Donegal Muster Roll]

MCDONALD, ARCHIBALD, mariner of the Broswell of Newport, Ireland, 1721. [NAS.AC8.260]

MCDONALD, JOHN, of Bornscitaik, was commissioned as a captain of Colonel Donald McDonald's regiment, Dublin, 1689. [NAS.RH4.90.7]

MCDONELL, Colonel ALEXANDER, formerly in the service of King Charles I, petitioned King Charles II for the return of his lands in 1661. [CSPIre]

MCDONELL, ALEXANDER, in Cooga, parish of Easky, County Sligo, 1665. [Hearth Tax Roll]

MCDONELL, ARCHIBALD, letter dated 1675. [PRONI.T640/126]

MCDONELL, ENEAS, in Bunnafeddy, parish of Dromard, County Sligo, 1665. [Hearth Tax Roll]

MCDONELL, JAMES, at the Catholic Camp of Ould Stoul, 1642. [NAS.GD406.1.1308]

MCDONELL, MILES, in Leacorrow, parish of Kilmachalgan, County Sligo, 1665. [Hearth Tax Roll]

MCDONELL, RANDELL, in Carrownrocly, parish of Easky, County Sligo, 1665. [Hearth Tax Roll]

MCDOUGALL, JAMES, of Garthland, to Ireland in 1645. [NAS.PA7.3.102]

MCDOWALL, ARCHIBALD, 14 October 1674. [NAS.RH15.91.40]

MCDOWELL, JANET, daughter of Uchtred McDowell the Provost of bangor, County Down, and spouse of William Barclay, 1616. [AG.IV.201]

MCFARLAN, DUNCAN, mustered with a sword and snaphance in the barony of Raphoe, County Donegal, 1630. [Donegal Muster Roll]

MCFARLAN, JOHN, mustered unarmed in the barony of
Raphoe, County Donegal, 1630. [Donegal Muster Roll]

MCFARLAN, JOHN, mustered with a sword and a callener in
the barony of Raphoe, County Donegal, 1630. [Donegal
Muster Roll]

MCFARLANE, MALCOLM, in the barony of
Magherasterhana and Clankeilly, County Fermanagh,
1631. [Fermanagh Muster Roll]

MCGHIE, GILBERT, a Covenanter and rebel, possibly from
Kirkcudbright, who fled to Ireland by 1684.
[RPCS.IX.344-381]

MCGIE, ARCHIBALD, a letter dated 1639.
[NAS.RH15.91.39]

MCGIE, ANTHONY, in Dungiven, County Londonderry,
1630. [Dungiven Muster Roll]

MCGIE, WILLIAM, from Kirkcudbright, a freeholder in
Ulster, 1620s. [NAS.RH15.91.33]

MCGILL, GEORGE, Captain of Home of the Heugh's
Regiment at Carrickfergus on 9 September 1642.
[DS#336]

MCGILL, HUGH, of Bellihornan, County Down, a charter
witness, 19 December 1661. [Laing#2554]

MCGILL, PHILIP, reference, 2 November 1698. [DP]

MCGOWAN, Cornet THOMAS, born 1618, died 16 March
1691. [Clogher Cathedral gravestone]

MACHAN, JOHN, in the parish of Raphoe, County Donegal,
1665. [HTR]

MCHUTCHEON, JOHN, in barony of Raphoe, 1630.
[Donegal Muster Roll]

MCILTHERNE, WILLIAM, mustered with a sword and callener in the barony of Raphoe, County Donegal, 1630. [Donegal Muster Roll]

MCILVAINE, ANDREW, mustered with a sword in the barony of Raphoe, County Donegal, 1630. [Donegal Muster Roll]

MCINTYRE, ROBERT, mustered with a sword and snaphance in the barony of Raphoe, Donegal, 1630. [Donegal Muster Roll]

MCKAINE, JOHN, mustered with a sword in the barony of Raphoe, County Donegal, 1630. [Donegal Muster Roll]

MCKASE, WILLIAM, mustered with a sword and snaphance in the barony of Raphoe, Donegal, 1630. [Donegal Muster Roll]

MCKEAG, THOMAS, mustered with a sword in the barony of Raphoe, County Donegal, 1630. [Donegal Muster Roll]

MCKEE, DONAL, mustered with sword and pike in the barony of Raphoe, County Donegal, 1630. [Donegal Muster Roll]

MCKEE, JOHN, mustered with sword and pike in the barony of Raphoe, County Donegal, 1630. [Donegal Muster Roll]

MCKEE, JOHN, mustered with a sword and halbert in the barony of Raphoe, County Donegal, 1630. [Donegal Muster Roll]

MCKEE, JOHN, mustered unarmed in the barony of Raphoe, County Donegal, 1630. [Donegal Muster Roll]

MCKEE, JOHN, a tenant on William Conyngham's lands in County Londonderry, 1683. [DP/Lenox-Conyngham pp]

MCKEE, WILLIAM, mustered with a sword in the barony of Raphoe, County Donegal, 1630. [Donegal Muster Roll]

MCKEEN, DONAL, mustered unarmed in the barony of Raphoe, County Donegal, 1630. [Donegal Muster Roll]

MCKEEN, JAMES, mustered with a sword in the barony of Raphoe, County Donegal, 1630. [Donegal Muster Roll]

MCKELVIE, NEALL, in the parish of Raphoe, County Donegal, 1665. [HTR]

MCKELVIE, WILLIAM, mustered with a sword in the barony of Raphoe, County Donegal, 1630. [Donegal Muster Roll]

MCKENRICK, GEORGE, in the barony of Magherasterhana and Clankeilly, County Fermanagh, 1631. [Fermanagh Muster Roll]

MACKIE, JAMES, in barony of Raphoe, 1630. [Donegal Muster Roll]

MCKILVANE, JOHN, mustered unarmed in the barony of Raphoe, County Donegal, 1630. [Donegal Muster Roll]

MCKINDLAY, DUNCAN, mustered with sword and pike in the barony of Raphoe, County Donegal, 1630. [Donegal Muster Roll]

MCKINDLAY, FYNDLEY, mustered with a sword in the barony of Raphoe, County Donegal, 1630. [Donegal Muster Roll]

MCKINDLAY, JOHN, the elder, mustered with a sword and pike in the barony of Raphoe, County Donegal, 1630. [Donegal Muster Roll]

MCKINDLAY, ROBERT, mustered with a sword in the barony of Raphoe, County Donegal, 1630. [Donegal Muster Roll]

MCLANY, HUMPHREY, mustered with a callener in the barony of Raphoe, County Donegal, 1630. [Donegal Muster Roll]

MCLEAN, Captain, ALLAN, of Balleny, Ireland, now in the Isle of Uist, 1714. [NAS.RD4.114.327]

MCMACHAN, ALEXANDER, mustered unarmed in the barony of Raphoe, County Donegal, 1630. [Donegal Muster Roll]

MCMAN, PATRICK, mustered with a sword in the barony of Raphoe, County Donegal, 1630. [Donegal Muster Roll]

MCMONGALL, DONELL, in the parish of Raphoe, County Donegal, 1665. [HTR]

MCMULLAN, ROBERT, in Anlow, County Londonderry, 9 August 1666. [NAS.RH15.91.40]

MCNAIR, OWEN, mustered with a sword and a pike in the barony of Raphoe, County Donegal, 1630. [Donegal Muster Roll]

MCNAUGHTON, PATRICK, and his wife, from Ireland, in Guthrie, Angus, in 1693. [NAS.CH2.535.1.303/67]

MCNEILL, DANIEL, in the Routt or the Glens of Antrim, a witness in 1661. [CSP.Ire.1661]

MCNEVIN, JOHN, mustered unarmed in the barony of Raphoe, County Donegal, 1630. [Donegal Muster Roll]

MCNEVIN, WILLIAM, mustered unarmed in the barony of Raphoe, County Donegal, 1630. [Donegal Muster Roll]

MCNEVIN, WILLIAM, in the parish of Raphoe, County Donegal, 1665. [HTR]

MCNICHOL, DONNELL, mustered with a sword and a pike in the barony of Raphoe, County Donegal, 1630. [Donegal Muster Roll]

MCPETER, DONAL, mustered unarmed in the barony of Raphoe, County Donegal, 1630. [Donegal Muster Roll]

MCPETER, ROBERT, mustered with a sword in the barony of Raphoe, County Donegal, 1630. [Donegal Muster Roll]

MCPHEDERS, ARCHIBALD, in the Routt or the Glens of Antrim, a witness in 1661. [CSP.Ire.1661]

MCQUILLING, RORY OGE, of Glenachartie, County Antrim, gentleman, and his wife Mary Nechterryse O'Neill, leased the lands of Tuissden from Archibald Edmonstone of Braidyland, on 8 May 1628. [NAS.GD97.Sec.1/390]

MCTYRE, ANDREW, mustered with a sword in the barony of Raphoe, County Donegal, 1630. [Donegal Muster Roll]

MCWILLIAM, ALEXANDER, mustered in the barony of Raphoe, County Donegal, 1630. [Donegal Muster Roll]

MARSHALL, STEPHEN, mustered with sword and snaphance in the barony of Raphoe, County Donegal, 1630. [Donegal Muster Roll]

MARSHALL, WILLIAM, mustered with sword and pike in the barony of Raphoe, County Donegal, 1630. [Donegal Muster Roll]

MARSHALL, WILLIAM, in the barony of Magheraboy, County Fermanagh, 1631. [Fermanagh Muster Roll]

MARTIN, JANET, daughter of John Martin a burgess of Irvine, and wife of Alexander Hobkin, miller at Bushmills, Ireland, 16 August 1615. [AG.VII.141]

MARTIN, THOMAS, yeoman in Corboylan, County Londonderry, lease, 1 June 1634. [PRONI.T640/35]

MARTIN, THOMAS, in Magiligan, County Londonderry, 9 August 1666. [NAS.RH15.91.40]

MATHEW, JOHN, mustered with sword and pike in the barony of Raphoe, County Donegal, 1630. [Donegal Muster Roll]

MATHEY, JAMES, mustered unarmed in the barony of Raphoe, County Donegal, 1630. [Donegal Muster Roll]

MATHIE, JAMES, mustered with a sword and snaphance in the barony of Raphoe, County Donegal, 1630. [Donegal Muster Roll]

MATTHY, ROBERT, in the parish of Raphoe, County Donegal, 1665. [HTR]

MAVOR, PHILLIP, an account dated December 1672. [NAS.RH15.91.40]

MAXWELL, ALEXANDER, an indenture dated 5 April 1655. [NAS.RH15.91.38]

MAXWELL, ALEXANDER, a gentleman, leased Dartries in the parish of Dunboe, County Londonderry, on 5 August 1655. [PRONI.T640/70]

MAXWELL, ANDREW, in Belfast, a letter dated 3 October 1672. [NAS.RH15.91.39]

MAXWELL, GABRIEL, mustered with a sword in the barony of Raphoe, County Donegal, 1630. [Donegal Muster Roll]

MAXWELL, or JOHNSTON, GABRIEL, a refugee from Scotland in Ireland 1670. [CSP.Ire]

MAXWELL, GEORGE, in Killeleagh near Downpatrick, 3 December 1672; 4 January 1676. [NAS.RH15.91.39][PRONI.T640/119/123]

MAXWELL, HENRY, in Inch, County Down, 1663. [PRONI.T640/96]

MAXWELL, HERBERT, of Dunconnell (?), a freeholder in
Ulster, 1620s. [NAS.RH15.91.33]

MAXWELL, JAMES, of Kirkconnell, renounced his interest
in the territory of Balligurgs, County Londonderry, on 27
February 1722. [NAS.NRAS#3323, bundle 20]

MAXWELL, JOHN, mustered with a sword and snaphance in
the barony of Raphoe, County Donegal, 1630. [Donegal
Muster Roll]

MAXWELL, JOHN, Lieutenant Colonel of Home of the
Heugh's Regiment at Carrickfergus on 9 September
1642. [DS#336]

MAXWELL, Lieutenant ROBERT, petitioned the Earl of
Strafford, Lord Lieutenant of Ireland, in 1638, and King
Charles I on 17 March 1638; an account dated 6
December 1639. [PRONI.T640/41][NAS.RH15.91.38]

MAXWELL, Sir ROBERT, of Ballycastle, County
Londonderry, 1661, 1666. [NAS.RH15.91.38/40]
[PRONI.T640/90]

MAXWELL, ROBERT, in Anlow, County Londonderry, 9
August 1666. [NAS.RH15.91.40]

MAXWELL, ROBERT, assignment with rental to James
Maxwell of Drum, 1674-1675. [PRONI.T640/120]

MAXWELL, ROBERT, in Dublin, a letter to George
Maxwell in Killeagh near Downpatrick, 3 December
1672. [PRONI.T640/119]

MAXWELL, THOMAS, a witness in Dungannon, County
Tyrone, 8 March 1667. [CSPIre]

MAXWELL, Sir WILLIAM, of Gubton (?), a freeholder in
Ulster, 1620s. [NAS.RH15.91.33]

MAXWELL, WILLIAM, a saddler in Killeleagh, 1672.
[NAS.RH15.91.39]

MEARS, JAMES, a merchant in Belfast, 1726.
  [NAS.AC9.967]

MELVILLE, ROBERT, Captain of the Earl of Leven's
  Regiment in Carrickfergus, 9 September 1642. [DS#328]

MENZIES, JOHN, mustered in the barony of Raphoe, County
  Donegal, 1630. [Donegal Muster Roll]

MENZIES, ROBERT, of Glassie, 22 February 1671.
  [NAS.NRAS234.BOX 74.2.77]

MIDDLETON, ALEXANDER, master of the Diligence of
  Dublin, 120 tons, trading to Spain in 1707.
  [NAS.GD220.6.1743]

MIDDLETON, Mrs, a tenant of William Conyngham in
  Armagh, 1683. [DP/Lenox-Conyngham pp]

MILLER, GEORGE, in Anlow, County Londonderry, 9
  August 1666. [NAS.RH15.91.40]

MILLER, HUGH, a burgess of Coleraine, 1659. [CSPIre]

MILLER, JAMES, a cooper in the Ards, Ireland, 1630. [see
  Janet Archibald's testament, confirmed 23 March 1630,
  Glasgow. NAS.CC9]

MILLER, JOHN, mustered with sword and pike in the barony
  of Raphoe, County Donegal, 1630. [Donegal Muster
  Roll]

MILLER, ROBERT, mustered unarmed in the barony of
  Raphoe, County Donegal, 1630. [Donegal Muster Roll]

MILLER, WILLIAM, mustered with sword and pike in the
  barony of Raphoe, County Donegal, 1630. [Donegal
  Muster Roll]

MILLER, the widow, in County Down, 1659.
  [NAS.RH15.91.38]

MILLIGAN, JOHN, the younger, mustered unarmed in the barony of Raphoe, County Donegal, 1630. [Donegal Muster Roll]

MILLIKEN, JAMES, a receipt dated 7 November 1672. [NAS.RH15.91.39][PRONI.T640/118]

MITCHELL, ALEXANDER, from Kirkcudbright, a freeholder in Ulster, 1620s. [NAS.RH15.91.33]

MIITCHELL, ANDREW, in the parish of Raphoe, County Donegal, 1665. [HTR]

MITCHELL, GAVIN, mustered with a sword in the barony of Raphoe, Donegal, 1630. [Donegal Muster Roll]

MITCHELL, JOHN, in County Fermanagh, 1631. [Fermanagh Muster Roll]

MITCHELL, JOHN, in the parish of Kilwaghter, 1652. [NAS.GD154.514]

MITCHELL, ROBERT, in County Fermanagh, 1631. [Fermanagh Muster Roll]

MITCHELL, ROBERT, [1], in the parish of Raphoe, County Donegal, 1665. [HTR]

MITCHELL, ROBERT, [2], in the parish of Raphoe, County Donegal, 1665. [HTR]

MITCHELL, WILLIAM, in Dungiven, County Londonderry, 1630. [Dungiven Muster Roll]

MITCHELL, WILLIAM, of Ardechilly, in the parish of Raphoe, County Donegal, 1665. [HTR]

MITCHELLBURNE, FRANCIS, in Killeleagh, 28 February 1673. [NAS.RH15.91.40]

MOFFAT, SIMON, in the barony of Magherasterhana and Clankeilly, County Fermanagh, 1631. [Fermanagh Muster Roll]

MOFFAT, WILLIAM, in the barony of Magherasterhana and Clankeilly, County Fermanagh, 1631. [Fermanagh Muster Roll]

MONCREIFF, JOHN, Captain of the Campbell of Lawers Regiment at Temple Patrick on 10 September 1642. [DS#335]

MONRO, ANDREW, son of General Robert Munro, petitioned King Charles II in 1660s. [CSPIre]

MONRO, GEORGE, Lieutenant Colonel of the Earl of Leven's Regiment in Carrickfergus, 9 September 1642. [DS#328]

MONRO, JOHN, Captain of Major General Robert Monro's Regiment in Carrickfergus on 9 September 1642. [DS#331]

MONRO, ROBERT, Colonel of Major General Robert Monro's Regiment in Carrickfergus on 9 September 1642. [DS#329]

MONTEITH, THOMAS, in Anlow, County Londonderry, 9 August 1666. [NAS.RH15.91.40]

MONTGOMERIE, Sir HUGH, of Newton, County Down, husband of Lady Elizabeth, an indenture dated 28 August 1610. (Sir Hugh died 15 May 1636, and Elizabeth, his wife, died 15 May 1623, both were buried in Newton kirk). A lease dated 22 August 1612 [Laing#1582] [PRONI.T640/3/6]

MONTGOMERIE, HUGH, of Knockokill, a letter dated 22 January 1654. [PRONI.T640/57]

MONTGOMERIE, HUGH, of Newton, a charter witness, 19 December 1661. [Laing#2554] a receipt dated 1672. [NAS.RH15.91.39]

MONTGOMERIE, Captain HUGH, clerk of His Majesty's stores, 1669. [NAS.RH15.91.38]

MONTGOMERIE, HUGH, in Dublin, 1670.
[NAS.GD3.5.607-717]

MONTGOMERIE, JOHN, of Cockilbie, was given a patent
of Indenization by King Charles I making him a free
native of Ireland, 7 June 1632. [Laing#2111]

MONTGOMERIE, JOHN, of Cockilbie, Stewarton, Ayrshire,
refers to his lands of Ballibuttle and Killivogane, Ireland,
in his testament written in August 1636, and confirmed
in Glasgow on 11 March 1648. [NAS.CC9]

MONTGOMERIE, WILLIAM, a writer burgess of Irvine but
residing in Donaghadee, County Down, husband of
Margaret Cunningham, disposed of his lands in Irvine
Ayrshire, 11 April 1620. [AG.IV.195]

MONTGOMERY, DUNCAN, mustered with a sword in the
barony of Raphoe, County Donegal, 1630. [Donegal
Muster Roll]

MONTGOMERY, HUGH, in the parish of Raphoe, County
Donegal, 1665. [HTR]

MONTGOMERY, JAMES, in the barony of Magherstefeny
(?), County Fermanagh, 1631. [Fermanagh Muster Roll]

MONTGOMERY, JAMES, Captain of the Earl of Eglinton's
Regiment in Bangor on 9 September 1642. [DS#333]

MONTGOMERY, JAMES, of Ballevely, County Antrim, a
Cornet, fought for King Charles II at Preston and at
Worcester, 1651, captured and shipped to Virginia,
returned to Ireland. [CSPIre.1661]

MONTGOMERY, JOHN, in Dungiven, County
Londonderry, 1630. [Dungiven Muster Roll]

MONTGOMERY, Cornet JOHN, of Ballievillie, petitioned
King Charles II in February 1661. [CSPIre]

MONTGOMERY, ROBERT, in Achinlurchare, County
Tyrone, 22 August 1612. [PRONI.T640]

MONTGOMERY, ROBERT, constable of Donnachdie,
Ireland, husband of Janet Harbert, 22 September 1620.
[NAS.RS11.1.539]

MONTGOMERY, ROBERT, mustered with a sword in the
barony of Raphoe, County Donegal, 1630. [Donegal
Muster Roll]

MONTGOMERY, ROBERT, Captain of the Earl of
Eglinton's Regiment in Bangor on 9 September 1642.
[DS#333]

MONTGOMERY, WILLIAM, a merchant in Dublin, 1714.
[NAS.AC9.493]

MONTGOMERY, Captain, of Craigbonnie, Donaghadee,
1715. [NAS.AC9.537]

MONYPENNY, ANDREW, clerk to the Archdeacon of
Connor, 1629. [NAS.GD97.Sec.1/398]

MOODY, JOHN, in the parish of Raphoe, County Donegal,
1665. [HTR]

MOORE, ALEXANDER, Captain of the Earl of Eglinton's
Regiment in Bangor on 9 September 1642. [DS#333]

MOORE, EUPHEMIA, 16.... [PRONI.T640A/4/5]

MOORE, JAMES, in the parish of Raphoe, County Donegal,
1665. [HTR]

MOORE, JAMES, of Ballybrogogh, County Down, executor
of William Moore of Glanderston, deceased in Scotland,
deed dated 13 May 1659; 1671; 15 November 1681.
[NAS.RH15.91.38][PRONI.T640/88/113; T640A/7]

MOORE, JAMES, in Ballydivity, 1725. [PRONI.D915/7/1]

MOORE, JOHN, mustered unarmed in the barony of Raphoe, County Donegal, 1630. [Donegal Muster Roll]

MOOREHEAD, WILLIAM, in Magiligan, County Londonderry, 9 August 1666. [NAS.RH15.91.40]

MORE, JOHN, mustered in the barony of Raphoe, County Donegal, 1630. [Donegal Muster Roll]

MORPHIE, ROGER, of Inniskillen, a tanner in County Fermanagh, 1722. [LI#405/406]

MORRISON, ALEXANDER, in the barony of Magheraboy, County Fermanagh, 1631. [Fermanagh Muster Roll]

MORRISON, GILBERT, mustered with a sword in the barony of Raphoe, County Donegal, 1630. [Donegal Muster Roll]

MORRISON, HERBERT, mustered with a sword and snaphance in the barony of Raphoe, Donegal, 1630. [Donegal Muster Roll]

MORRISON, JAMES, mustered with a sword and pike in the barony of Raphoe, County Donegal, 1630. [Donegal Muster Roll]

MORRISON, JAMES, mustered unarmed in the barony of Raphoe, County Donegal, 1630. [Donegal Muster Roll]

MORRISON, JAMES, a tenant, 1663. [NAS.RH15.91.38C]

MORRISON, JOHN, mustered unarmed in the barony of Raphoe, County Donegal, 1630. [Donegal Muster Roll]

MORRISON, JOSEPH, a merchant in Londonderry, 1707, 1711. [NAS.AC10.64; AC13.1.124]

MORRISON, RICHARD, master of the Northbore of Londonderry in 1705. [CalSPDom.SP42/120/61]

MORRISON, ROBERT, mustered with a sword and a pike in the barony of Raphoe, County Donegal, 1630. [Donegal Muster Roll]

MORRISON, ROBERT, a tenant, 1663. [NAS.RH15.91.38C]

MORRISON, ROBERT, of Bellykoly, in the parish of Raphoe, County Donegal, 1665. [HTR]

MORTON, WILLIAM, Captain of the Earl of Lindsay's Regiment at Carrickfergus in September 1642. [DS#334]

MOWBRAY, ARTHUR, mustered with a sword in the barony of Raphoe, County Donegal, 1630. [Donegal Muster Roll]

MOY, HERO, a merchant in Londonderry, 1710. [NAS.AC9.351]

MUIRHEAD, WILLIAM, a saddler in Antrim, husband of Isobel Lang, disposed of the chapel yard of Balquouran in favour of Archibald Edmonstone of Duntreath, 13 September 1676. [NAS.GD97.Sec.1/540]

MUNDELL, JOHN, in the barony of Magherasterhana and Clankeilly, County Fermanagh, 1631. [Fermanagh Muster Roll]

MUNRO, JOHN, in the parish of Kilwaghter, 1652. [NAS.GD154.514]

MURE, ALEXANDER, receipts for victualling in Carrickfergus, 1641-1643. [NAS.PA7.III/6]

MURE, GAVIN, in the parish of Kilwaghter, 1652. [NAS.GD154.514]

MURE, HUGH, mustered with sword and halbert in the barony of Raphoe, County Donegal, 1630. [Donegal Muster Roll]

MURE, JAMES, in Ballybregagh, County Down, 24 July 1674, 1684. [PRONI.T640/121/136]

MURE, MARGARET, relict of Henry Walker mason in
Maybole, Ayrshire, and spouse of Ludovick Stewart in
Ireland, 30 June 1634. [NAS.RS11.6.226]

MURE, QUINTIN, from Irvine but resident in Coleraine,
County Londonderry, husband of Margaret Hendrie,
disposed of property in Irvine on 18 June 1618.
[AG.IV.30]

MURE, WILLIAM, sometime in Cumbria then in Ireland,
debtor to Hugh Costein a merchant burgess of Dumfries,
1639.   [NAS.CC5.6.2/51]

MURRAY, ALEXANDER, in the parish of Raphoe, County
Donegal, 1665. [HTR]

MURRAY, GEORGE, a refugee from Limerick, 1689.
[NAS.CH2.635.1/59]

MURRAY, GIDEON, Captain of the Earl of Lothian's
Regiment in Carrickfergus on 9 September 1642.
[DS#329]

MURRAY, JOHN, Earl of Annandale, was granted the lands
of Boylagh and Bannagh, County Donegal, 8 February
1627. [Laing#1984]

MURRAY, Sir JOHN, Captain of the Earl of Lothian's
Regiment in Carrickfergus on 9 September 1642.
[DS#329]

MURRAY, JOHN, son and heir of Richard Murray of
Broughton and his wife Anna, purchased the lands of
Killibeggs, barony of Boylagh and Banagh, County
Donegal, 20 January 1698. [Laing#2968]

MURRAY, KATHERINE, wife of Alexander Cunningham
minister at Kirkinver, Donegal, 6 July 1621, 17 June
1622, and 23 September 1625; wife of Alexander
Cunningham the Dean of Rapho, Ireland, 27 June 1636
and 1 November 1659. [NAS.RS11.2.171/174/
331/332/425; RS11.6.482; RS11.9.478]

MURRAY, MUNGO, was granted the lands of Bonneglen or
Drumachquhen, County Donegal, in August 1641.
[Laing#2293]

MURRAY, MUNGO, Captain of the Earl of Lindsay's
Regiment at Carrickfergus in September 1642. [DS#334]

MURRAY, RICHARD, mustered in the barony of Raphoe,
County Donegal, 1630. [Donegal Muster Roll]

MURRAY, RICHARD, in County Fermanagh, 1631.
[Fermanagh Muster Roll]

MURRAY, RICHARD, a witness, 26 August 1656.
[NAS.RH15.91.38]

MURRAY, RICHARD, a deposition dated after 1663.
[PRONI.T640/100]

MURRAY, RICHARD, Captain of a militia troop of horse in
County Donegal, 1678. [NAS.GD10.1380]

MURRAY, RICHARD, owner of the Joseph of Londonderry,
1721. [NAS.AC9.786]

MURRAY, THOMAS, in the parish of Raphoe, County
Donegal, 1665. [HTR]

MURRAY, WILLIAM, in the barony of Magherasterhana and
Clankeilly, County Fermanagh, 1631. [Fermanagh
Muster Roll]

MYLNE, ANDREW, Lieutenant Colonel of the Campbell of
Lawers Regiment at Temple Patrick on 10 September
1642. [DS#335]

NAPIER, DOROTHY, a widow in Loughcrow, County
Meath, probate 1690 PCC

NEALSON, JAMES, mustered with a sword in the barony of
Raphoe, County Donegal, 1630. [Donegal Muster Roll]

NEEDHAM, THOMAS, a merchant in Dublin, 1704.
[NAS.AC9.97]

NEILSON, ROBERT, an assizeman in Dungannon, County
Tyrone, 8 March 1667. [CSPIre]

NESBIT, JAMES, mustered unarmed in the barony of
Raphoe, County Donegal, 1630. [Donegal Muster Roll]

NEVIN, JAMES, in the parish of Raphoe, County Donegal,
1665. [HTR]

NICOLL, JOHN, in Magiligan, County Londonderry, 9
August 1666. [NAS.RH15.91.40]

NICOLSON, JOHN, tenant, 1669. [NAS.RH15.91.38A]

NISBET, ALEXANDER, of Cornigilligh, in the parish of
Raphoe, County Donegal, 1665. [HTR]

NISBET, GEORGE, in the parish of Raphoe, County
Donegal, 1665. [HTR]

NISBET, HUGH, in the parish of Raphoe, County Donegal,
1665. [HTR]

NISBET, JOHN, of Tullidonell, in the parish of Raphoe,
County Donegal, 1665. [HTR]

NISBET, ROBERT, in the parish of Raphoe, County Donegal,
1665. [HTR]

NIVEN, HUGH, tenant, May 1672. [NAS.RH15.91.40]

NOBLE, QUINTIN, in the barony of Magherasterhana and
Clankeilly, County Fermanagh, 1631. [Fermanagh
Muster Roll]

NOBLE, WILLIAM, mustered unarmed in the barony of
Raphoe, County Donegal, 1630. [Donegal Muster Roll]

OGLE, ALEXANDER, in the barony of Magheraboy, County
Fermanagh, 1631. [Fermanagh Muster Roll]

OLIVER, JAMES, in Dungiven, County Londonderry, 1630.
[Dungiven Muster Roll]

ORR, ALEXANDER, in the parish of Raphoe, County
Donegal, 1665. [HTR]

ORR, JOHN, a servant in Gallanagh, parish of Urney, County
Tyrone, 1660. [Poll Tax Returns]

OSBURNE, ALEXANDER, late in Montgomeriestoun,
Ayrshire, a minister in Dublin, 1665. [NAS.GD1.521.24]

OSBURNE, MARION, daughter of John Osburne in Bert,
Donegal, and spouse of Laurence Legaitt, son of Thomas
Legaitt portioner of Warriks, 29 December 1631.
[NAS.RS11.5.215]

PATON, JAMES, in the parish of Raphoe, County Donegal,
1665. [HTR]

PATON, JOHN, of Maghricoren, in the parish of Raphoe,
County Donegal, 1665. [HTR]

PATON, WILLIAM, minister at Rathmoithie, 1616.
[AG.VII.67]

PATTEN, ALEXANDER, in Anlow, County Londonderry, 9
August 1666. [NAS.RH15.91.40]

PATTEN, ARCHIBALD, in Dungiven, County Londonderry,
1630. [Dungiven Muster Roll]

PATTEN, ROGER, in Dungiven, County Londonderry, 1630.
[Dungiven Muster Roll]

PATTEN,...., in Magiligan, County Londonderry, 9 August
1666. [NAS.RH15.91.40]

PATTERSON, ALEXANDER, in the barony of Magheraboy,
County Fermanagh, 1631. [Fermanagh Muster Roll]

PATTERSON, ELIZABETH, daughter of James Patterson in Greengraves, parish of Newtown, County Down, formerly in Langnewtoun, Roxburghshire, 1691. [NAS.RD3.LXXIV.278]

PATTERSON, JAMES, mustered with sword and pike in the barony of Raphoe, County Donegal, 1630. [Donegal Muster Roll]

PATTERSON, JANET, daughter of James Patterson in Greengraves, parish of Newtown, County Down, formerly in Langnewtoun, Roxburghshire, 1691. [NAS.RD3.LXXIV.278]

PATTERSON, JOHN, mustered with a sword in the barony of Raphoe, County Donegal, 1630. [Donegal Muster Roll]

PATTERSON, JOHN, mustered with sword and pike in the barony of Raphoe, County Donegal, 1630. [Donegal Muster Roll]

PATTERSON, JOHN, in the parish of Raphoe, County Donegal, 1665. [HTR]

PATTERSON, MATTHEW, mustered with a sword in the barony of Raphoe, County Donegal, 1630. [Donegal Muster Roll]

PEACOCK, JOHN, in County Down, 1610. [Laing#1582]

PEACOCK, JOHN, mustered unarmed in the barony of Raphoe, County Donegal, 1630. [Donegal Muster Roll]

PEACOCK, MORRIS, mustered unarmed in the barony of Raphoe, County Donegal, 1630. [Donegal Muster Roll]

PEDEN, ALEXANDER, a refugee from Scotland in Ireland 1670. [CSP.Ire]

PEEBLES, HUGH, in the parish of Kilwaghter, 1652. [NAS.GD154.514]

PEEBLES, JOHN, of Pethirland, afterwards in Tollochgoir, Antrim, 21 July 1625, later in the parish of Balliemoney, Ireland, 15 November 1632. [NAS.RS11.3.372; RS11.4.58; RS11.5.327]

PEEBLES, JOHN, the younger, of Tullagorra, Antrim, 1 June 1627. [NAS.RS27.4.58]

PEIRSON, DAVID, in County Donegal, 1693. [NAS.GD1.510.112]

PERRY, ALEXANDER, in the parish of Raphoe, County Donegal, 1665. [HTR]

PERRY, ..., a widow, in the parish of Raphoe, County Donegal, 1665. [HTR]

PIPER, JAMES, of Coradale, aged 50, a witness, 26 August 1656. [NAS.RH15.91.38]

PIRRY, JOHN, mustered with a sword and snaphance in the barony of Raphoe, County Donegal, 1630. [Donegal Muster Roll]

PIRRY, THOMAS, an assizeman in Dungannon, County Tyrone, 8 March 1667. [CSPIre]

PITSCOTTIE, COLIN, Lieutenant Colonel of the Earl of Eglinton's Regiment in Bangor on 9 September 1642. [DS#333]

PITTY, JOHN, mustered unarmed in the barony of Raphoe, County Donegal, 1630. [Donegal Muster Roll]

POAK, ROBERT, in the parish of Raphoe, County Donegal, 1665. [HTR]

PORTER, JAMES, tenant on William Conyngham's lands in County Londonderry, 1683. [DP/Lenox-Conyngham pp]

PORTER, JOHN, mustered unarmed in the barony of Raphoe, County Donegal, 1630. [Donegal Muster Roll]

PORTER, PATRICK, mustered unarmed in the barony of Raphoe, County Donegal, 1630. [Donegal Muster Roll]

PORTER, PATRICK, mustered with a sword and snaphance in the barony of Raphoe, County Donegal, 1630. [Donegal Muster Roll]

PORTER, WILLIAM, mustered unarmed in the barony of Raphoe, County Donegal, 1630. [Donegal Muster Roll]

PORTER, WILLIAM, in the barony of Magherasterhana and Clankeilly, County Fermanagh, 1631. [Fermanagh Muster Roll]

POUCK, JOHN, in the parish of Raphoe, County Donegal, 1665. [HTR]

PRINGLE, JEAN, spouse of William Kilpatrick in Ireland, 1697. [NAS.RD3.87.248]

PROVAN, THOMAS, born 1618, late of Augher, died 13 August 1705. [Clogher Cathedral gravestone]

PURVEYANCE, ELIZABETH, daughter of John Purveyance in Machribeg, Ireland, formerly in Huingriehill, 2 June 1625; later spouse of Archibald Baidie in Gortinerall, Ireland, 15 June 1633. [NAS.RS11.3.336; 6.31]

PURVEYANCE, JOHN, in Machribeg, Ireland, formerly in Huingriehill, 2 June 1625. [NAS.RS11.3.336]

RAE, ROBERT, mustered with a sword in the barony of Raphoe, County Donegal, 1630. [Donegal Muster Roll]

RAE, ROBERT, mustered unarmed in the barony of Raphoe, County Donegal, 1630. [Donegal Muster Roll]

RAINE, WILLIAM, a merchant in Belfast, 1722. [NAS.AC9.849]

RALSTON, JOHN, mustered with a sword in the barony of Raphoe, County Donegal, 1630. [Donegal Muster Roll]

RAMSAY, DANIEL, mustered with a sword and snaphance in the barony of Raphoe, County Donegal, 1630. [Donegal Muster Roll]

RAMSAY, DAVID, mustered with a sword and snaphance in the barony of Raphoe, Donegal, 1630. [Donegal Muster Roll]

RAMSAY, DAVID, receipt dated 1662. [NAS.RH15.91.40]

RAMSAY, HUGH, tenant on William Cunningham's lands in County Londonderry, 1683. [DP/Lenox-Conyngham pp]

RAMSAY, THOMAS, mustered with a sword in the barony of Raphoe, County Donegal, 1630. [Donegal Muster Roll]

RAMSAY, THOMAS, of Findram, in the parish of Raphoe, County Donegal, 1665. [HTR]

RANKIN, COSTYNE, mustered with a sword in the barony of Raphoe, County Donegal, 1630. [Donegal Muster Roll]

RANKIN, GEORGE, in the barony of Magheraboy, County Fermanagh, 1631. [Fermanagh Muster Roll]

RANKIN, GEORGE, in the parish of Raphoe, County Donegal, 1665. [HTR]

RANKIN, JAMES, in barony of Raphoe, 1630. [Donegal Muster Roll]

RANKIN, JOHN, in the parish of Raphoe, County Donegal, 1665. [HTR]

RANKIN, NATHANIEL, of Grimport, Ireland, master of the Sara of Belfast, 1721. [NAS.AC9.757]

RANKIN, WILLIAM, mustered with a sword and snaphance in the barony of Raphoe, County Donegal, 1630. [Donegal Muster Roll]

RANKIN, WILLIAM, mustered unarmed in the barony of Raphoe, County Donegal, 1630. [Donegal Muster Roll]

READ, ALEXANDER, son of Michael Read in Ireland, was admitted as a burgess of Stirling on 18 January 1654. [Stirling Burgess Roll]

READ, JAMES, in Lisburn 1672. [NAS.RH15.91.39]

REEKIE, JAMES, in the barony of Magheraboy, County Fermanagh, 1631. [Fermanagh Muster Roll]

REID, DAVID, mustered with a sword in the barony of Raphoe, County Donegal, 1630. [Donegal Muster Roll]

REID, GEORGE, in the barony of Magherasterhana and Clankeilly, County Fermanagh, 1631. [Fermanagh Muster Roll]

REID, HUGH, mustered unarmed in the barony of Raphoe, County Donegal, 1630. [Donegal Muster Roll]

REID, JAMES, in Belligrottis, Ireland, formerly in Willockshill, 12 January 1625.[NAS.RS11.3.241]

REID, JOHN, the elder, in County Down, 1659. [NAS.RH15.91.38]

REID, JOHN, the younger, in Ballehamlin, 1659. [NAS.RH15.91.38]

REID, ROBERT, receipt dated 1662. [NAS.RH15.91.40]

REID, THOMAS, in Meochill, parish of Achadowy, County Londonderry, contract with Hugh Thompson, flesher burgess of Irvine, 14 August 1665. [NAS.GD1.693.11]

REID, WILLIAM, receipt dated 1662. [NAS.RH15.91.40]

REID, WILLIAM. Petition by Robert Fergushill of Burnockstoun on behalf of his father in law William Reid of Dardilling, minister at Ballywalter, Ireland, against James Crawford of Ardmillan and Hugh Crawford, merchant in Ayr, 13 August 1690. [NAS.PAY.77]

RENWICK, JOHN, in the barony of Magheraboy, County Fermanagh, 1631. [Fermanagh Muster Roll]

RENWICK, WALTER, in the barony of Magherstefeny (?), County Fermanagh, 1631. [Fermanagh Muster Roll]

RICHARDSON, JAMES, an assizeman in Dungannon, County Tyrone, 8 March 1667. [CSPIre]

RICHARDSON, W., an assizeman in Dungannon, County Tyrone, 8 March 1667. [CSPIre]

RICHIE, JAMES, mustered with a sword and a pike in the barony of Raphoe, County Donegal, 1630. [Donegal Muster Roll]

RICHIE, JOHN, mustered with sword and pike in the barony of Raphoe, County Donegal, 1630. [Donegal Muster Roll]

RICHIE, WILLIAM, mustered with a sword in the barony of Raphoe, 1630. [Donegal Muster Roll]

RICHMOND, ANDREW, in the parish of Raphoe, County Donegal, 1665. [HTR]

RICHMONT, MARGARET, daughter of Robert Richmont in Parkerstoun, and spouse of Alexander Broun in Inchoan, Donegal, Ireland, 15 June 1627. [NAS.RS11.4.67]

RIDDELL, JAMES, Major of the Earl of Lothian's Regiment in Carrickfergus on 9 September 1642. [DS#329]

RIDDELL, Sir WALTER, Captain of the Earl of Lothian's Regiment in Carrickfergus on 9 September 1642. [DS#329]

ROBERTSON, JAMES, son of George Robertson in Limnavadie, Londonderry, 12 July 1633, and 27 November 1633. [NAS.RS11.6.58/107]

ROBERTSON, ROBERT, mustered unarmed in the barony of Raphoe, County Donegal, 1630. [Donegal Muster Roll]

ROBERTSON, WILLIAM, Cornet of the Royal Dragoons of Ireland, 1721, son of Colin Robertson, son of Gilbert Robertson of Kindeace. [NAS.RS38.VIII.34/60/62; IX.304]

ROBINSON, ARCHIBALD, of Paveclogh, in the parish of Raphoe, County Donegal, 1665. [HTR]

ROBINSON, HUGH, in the parish of Raphoe, County Donegal, 1665. [HTR]

ROBINSON, JAMES, mustered with sword and pike in the barony of Raphoe, County Donegal, 1630. [Donegal Muster Roll]

ROBINSON, ROBERT, mustered unarmed in the barony of Raphoe, County Donegal, 1630. [Donegal Muster Roll]

ROBINSON, ROBERT, in the parish of Raphoe, County Donegal, 1665. [HTR]

ROBINSON, SAMUEL, chaplain, witness to a deed of factory at Redhall, County Antrim, 25 November 1729. [NAS.GD97.Sec.1/677]

ROBISON, JOHN, merchant in Killelagh, County Down, 1671. [NAS.RH15.91.38][PRONI.T640/111]

ROGER, ALEXANDER, in Dungiven, County Londonderry, 1630. [Dungiven Muster Roll]

ROGER, ANDREW, in the parish of Raphoe, County Donegal, 1665. [HTR]

ROGER, GEORGE, in the parish of Raphoe, County Donegal, 1665. [HTR]

ROGER, JOHN, mustered unarmed in the barony of Raphoe, County Donegal, 1630. [Donegal Muster Roll]

ROGER, JOHN, mustered unarmed in the barony of Raphoe, County Donegal, 1630. [Donegal Muster Roll]

ROGER, JOHN, in the parish of Raphoe, County Donegal, 1665. [HTR]

ROGER, ROBERT, mustered unarmed in the barony of Raphoe, County Donegal, 1630. [Donegal Muster Roll]

ROGER, THOMAS, in the parish of Raphoe, County Donegal, 1665. [HTR]

ROGER, WALTER, mustered unarmed in the barony of Raphoe, County Donegal, 1630. [Donegal Muster Roll]

ROSS, GAVIN, a yeoman in Ardutigall, Londonderry, a bond, 1624. [PRONI.T640/24]

ROSS, GEORGE, of Galston, parish of Avondale, probably a Covenanting refugee, to Ireland by 1683. [RPCS.VIII.653]

ROSS, GEORGE, of Galstrich, owner of the lands of Broomhill, Barony parish of Glasgow, probably a Covenanting refugee, to Ireland by 1683. [RPCS.VIII.644]

ROSS, JAMES, a wright burgess of Bangour, son of Alexander Ross a wright burgess of Irvine, Ayrshire, 1620. [AG.IX.276]

ROSS, JAMES, in County Fermanagh, 1631. [Fermanagh Muster Roll]

ROSS, JOHN, in Dungiven, County Londonderry, 1630. [Dungiven Muster Roll]

ROSS, JOHN, in Ireland, letter dated 17 January 1683. [NAS.RH15.39.18]

ROSS, Mrs SARAH, from Ireland to Portpatrick in May 1693. [EUL.Laing.490/123/4]

ROSS, WILLIAM, from Ross Isle, Scotland, a Member of the
Irish Parliament, petitioned King Charles II in
1662/1663. [CSPIre]

ROUCHE, JOHN, Captain of Lord Sinclair's Regiment in
Newry on 28 September 1642. [DS#337]

ROY, JOHN, in Anlow, County Londonderry, 9 August 1666.
[NAS.RH15.91.40]

RUSSELL, ALEXANDER, in the parish of Kilwaghter, 1652.
[NAS.GD154.514]

SALMOND, HUGH, mustered unarmed in the barony of
Raphoe, County Donegal, 1630. [Donegal Muster Roll]

SANDALL, JOHN, in Belfast, 16... [NAS.GD406.1.10667]

SANDERSON, THOMAS, an assizeman in Dungannon,
County Tyrone, 8 March 1667. [CSPIre]

SANDERSON, THOMAS, in the barony of Magheraboy,
County Fermanagh, 1631. [Fermanagh Muster Roll]

SCALES, JAMES, tenant on William Conyngham's estate in
County Londonderry, 1683. [DP/Lenox-Conyngham pp]

SCHAW, JOHN, of Greenock, was given a patent of
Indenization by King Charles I making him a free native
of Ireland, 7 June 1632. [Laing#2111]

SCHAW, WILLIAM, was given a patent of Indenization by
King Charles I making him a free native of Ireland, 7
June 1632. [Laing#2111]

SCOTT, ARCHIBALD, in the barony of Magherasterhana
and Clankeilly, County Fermanagh, 1631. [Fermanagh
Muster Roll]

SCOTT, DAVID, in the barony of Magherstefeny (?), County
Fermanagh, 1631. [Fermanagh Muster Roll]

SCOTT, DAVID, of Bargansholme, parish of Old Monkland, probably a Covenanting refugee, to Ireland by 1683. [RPCS.VIII.642]

SCOTT, GEORGE, mustered with a sword and pike in the barony of Raphoe, County Donegal, 1630. [Donegal Muster Roll]

SCOTT, JAMES, mustered with a sword and snaphance in the barony of Raphoe, County Donegal, 1630. [Donegal Muster Roll]

SCOTT, JAMES, in Anlow, County Londonderry, 9 August 1666. [NAS.RH15.91.40]

SCOTT, JOHN, mustered with a sword in the barony of Raphoe, County Donegal, 1630. [Donegal Muster Roll]

SCOTT, JOHN, in Anlow, County Londonderry, 9 August 1666. [NAS.RH15.91.40]

SCOTT, JOSEPH, a gentleman in Drogheda then in London, probate 1688 PCC

SCOTT, MATTHEW, master of the Upton of Belfast, from Ireland to Catalonia in December 1705. [CalSPDom.SP42/119/193]

SCOTT, ROBERT, in County Fermanagh, 1631. [Fermanagh Muster Roll]

SCOTT, WALTER, Lieutenant Colonel of the Earl of Lothian's Regiment in Carrickfergus on 9 September 1642. [DS#329]

SCOTT, WILLIAM, mustered with a sword in the barony of Raphoe, County Donegal, 1630. [Donegal Muster Roll]

SCOTT, WILLIAM, in the barony of Magheraboy, County Fermanagh, 1631. [Fermanagh Muster Roll]

SCOTT, WILLIAM, tenant farmer in Ballymaglane Itragh, barony of Kinelarty, County Down, 1703. [PRONI.D1854/2/29A]

SEATOUN, DAVID, Captain of Lord Sinclair's Regiment in Newry on 28 September 1642. [DS#337]

SELIMAN, THOMAS, in the parish of Kilwaghter, 1652. [NAS.GD154.514]

SEMPLE, Sir BRYCE, 7 August 1641. [NAS.GD2/22]

SEMPLE, GABRIEL, a refugee from Scotland in Ireland 1670. [CSP.Ire]

SEMPLE, JOHN, a mariner from Carrickfergus who died on the America in Jamaica, probate 1694 PCC

SEMPLE, WILLIAM, 1624-1674, a Presbyterian minister in Letterkenny, a letter dated Dublin 15 March 1672. [NLS.Wod.Fol.XXVI.221]; a non-conformist minister who had been imprisoned for seven years in Lifford gaol, petitioned King Charles II for his release, 1669. [CSPIre]

SHANNAN, GEORGE, a carpenter on the Ringsell of Dublin, 1715; a shipbuilder in Dublin, 1716. [NAS.AC9.581]

SHAW, HUGH, of Ballynamanagh, witness, 26 August 1656. [NAS.RH15.91.38]

SHAW, JOHN, a Presbyterian minister at Ahoghill, died 1674, a letter dated Mabuie in March 1672. [NLS.Wod.Fol.XXVI/222]

SHAW, PATRICK, of Ballywalter, 28 August 1610. [Laing#1582]

SHAW, ROBERT, a trader to Ireland, 1714. [NAS.RD2.103/2.110]

SHAW, W., in Newton, Ireland, 1645. [NLS.Wod.Fol.XXV/52]

SHEARER, KATHERINE, tenant, 1663.
[NAS.RH15.91.38D]

SHIELLS, JAMES, of Figert, in the parish of Raphoe, County
Donegal, 1665. [HTR]

SIME, MARGARET, *'ane uther Scottis Irish gentlewoman'*,
with children, whose husband had been killed by the
Irish rebels, refugees in Elgin, Morayshire, by 1643.
[Elgin KSR]

SIMPSON, JOHN, in the barony of Magherasterhana and
Clankeilly, County Fermanagh, 1631. [Fermanagh
Muster Roll]

SIMSON, FRANCIS, a surgeon, probably from Belfast, who
died aboard HMS Martha at Bengal, probate 1696 PCC

SIMSON, JOHN, from Belfast, a surgeon aboard the Edward
and Francis of London, probate 1694 PCC

SINCLAIR, HENRY, Lieutenant Colonel of Lord Sinclair's
Regiment in Newry on 28 September 1642. [DS#337]

SINCLAIR, PATRICK, Captain of Lord Sinclair's Regiment
in Newry on 28 September 1642. [DS#337]

SLOAN, ALEXANDER, 1659. [NAS.RH15.91.38]

SLOMAN, GEORGE, a carpenter in Dublin, 1715.
[NAS.AC9.558; AC8.185]

SMALL, ROBERT, in Magiligan, County Londonderry, 9
August 1666. [NAS.RH15.91.40]

SMEALLY, JOHN, mustered in the barony of Raphoe,
County Donegal, 1630. [Donegal Muster Roll]

SMEALLY, ROBERT, mustered with sword and musket in
the barony of Raphoe, County Donegal, 1630. [Donegal
Muster Roll]

SMITH, GILBERT, in Anlow, County Londonderry, 9
August 1666. [NAS.RH15.91.40]

SMITH, JOHN, of Knockegarran, in the parish of Raphoe,
County Donegal, 1665. [HTR]

SMITH, ROBERT, in the barony of Magherstefeny (?),
County Fermanagh, 1631. [Fermanagh Muster Roll]

SMITH, ROBERT, in the parish of Raphoe, County Donegal,
1665. [HTR]

SMITH, ROBERT, of Gorrequigly, in the parish of Raphoe,
County Donegal, 1665. [HTR]

SMITH, WILLIAM, alderman and merchant of Londonderry,
1689, in Ayr 1690. [NAS.RH15.112/2/55, 65, 79]

SMITH, WILLIAM, of Edernie, County Fermanagh, 1721.
[NAS.AC8.260]

SMYTH, JOHN, mustered with a sword in the barony of
Raphoe, County Donegal, 1630. [Donegal Muster Roll]

SNODGRASS, JOHN, mustered with a sword and a pike in
the barony of Raphoe, County Donegal, 1630. [Donegal
Muster Roll]

SNODGRASS, JOHN, mustered unarmed in the barony of
Raphoe, County Donegal, 1630. [Donegal Muster Roll]

SNODGRASS, ROBERT, of Beltany, in the parish of Raphoe,
County Donegal, 1665. [HTR]

SOMERVILLE, ROBERT, in the barony of Magherstefeny
(?), County Fermanagh, 1631. [Fermanagh Muster Roll]

SOMERVILLE, ..., a witness, 1695. [NAS.RH15.91.39]

SPENCE, ALEXANDER, in the barony of Magheraboy,
County Fermanagh, 1631. [Fermanagh Muster Roll]

SPENCE, DUNCAN, mustered with a sword in the barony of Raphoe, County Donegal, 1630. [Donegal Muster Roll]

SPENCE, JOHN, in the barony of Magheraboy, County Fermanagh, 1631. [Fermanagh Muster Roll]

SPENCE, THOMAS, in the barony of Magheraboy, County Fermanagh, 1631. [Fermanagh Muster Roll]

SPITTAL, ALEXANDER, an account dated 1672. [NAS.RH15.91.39]

SPREULL, ARCHIBALD, in the parish of Raphoe, County Donegal, 1665. [HTR]

SPREULL, JAMES, mustered with a sword and pike in the barony of Raphoe, County Donegal, 1630. [Donegal Muster Roll]

SPREULL, JOHN, of Stranorlaghan, in the parish of Raphoe, County Donegal, 1665. [HTR]

STARRET, ALEXANDER, mustered with a sword in the barony of Raphoe, County Donegal, 1630. [Donegal Muster Roll]

STARRET, JAMES, in the parish of Raphoe, County Donegal, 1665. [HTR]

STARRET, PETER, mustered with sword and pike in the barony of Raphoe, County Donegal, 1630. [Donegal Muster Roll]

STARRET, ROBERT, mustered with a sword in the barony of Raphoe, County Donegal, 1630. [Donegal Muster Roll]

STARRET, WILLIAM, mustered unarmed in the barony of Raphoe, County Donegal, 1630. [Donegal Muster Roll]

STEILL, JAMES, mustered with sword and pike in the barony of Raphoe, County Donegal, 1630. [Donegal Muster Roll]

STEPHEN, ANDREW, mustered unarmed in the barony of Raphoe, County Donegal, 1630. [Donegal Muster Roll]

STEPHEN, JOHN, mustered with a sword and pike in the barony of Raphoe, County Donegal, 1630. [Donegal Muster Roll]

STEPHENSON, ALEXANDER, in Dungiven, County Londonderry, 1630. [Dungiven Muster Roll]

STEPHENSON, ANDREW, mustered with a sword in the barony of Raphoe, County Donegal, 1630. [Donegal Muster Roll]

STEPHENSON, GEORGE, mustered with a sword in the barony of Raphoe, County Donegal, 1630. [Donegal Muster Roll]

STEPHENSON, JAMES, tenant on William Conyngham's lands in County Londonderry, 1683. [DP/Lenox-Conyngham pp]

STEPHENSON, JOHN, mustered unarmed in the barony of Raphoe, County Donegal, 1630. [Donegal Muster Roll]

STEPHENSON, JOHN, and his wife Anne, 1682. [NAS.RH15.91.40]

STEPHENSON, THOMAS, tenant on William Conyngham's lands in County Londonderry, 1683. [DP/Lenox-Conyngham pp]

STEVENSON, JAMES, in Anlow, County Londonderry, 9 August 1666. [NAS.RH15.91.40]

STEVENSON, JOHN, mustered unarmed in the barony of Raphoe, County Donegal, 1630. [Donegal Muster Roll]

STEVENSON, JOHN, mustered with a sword and snaphance in the barony of Raphoe, County Donegal, 1630. [Donegal Muster Roll]

STEVENSON, ROBERT, a burgess of Irvine but residing in Raphoe, Ireland, husband of Elizabeth Dunlop sister of John Dunlop who died in Irvine during 1615. [AG.VII.212]

STEVENSON, ROBERT, in the parish of Raphoe, County Donegal, 1665. [HTR]

STEVENSON, THOMAS, of Culladery, in the parish of Raphoe, County Donegal, 1665. [HTR]

STEVENSON, THOMAS, in Anlow, County Londonderry, 9 August 1666. [NAS.RH15.91.40]

STEVENSON, WILLIAM, mustered with sword and pike in the barony of Raphoe, County Donegal, 1630. [Donegal Muster Roll]

STEWART, Sir ANDREW, of Castle Stewart, County Tyrone, conveyance to Anne, widow of John Boyes in County Tyrone, of the lands of Drumconfosse, Mulloghtetory, Balliolargan, Turble and Coagh, dated 1 November 1630. [DP/Lenox-Conyngham pp]

STEWART, ANDREW, of Tierarly, County Armagh, leased the townland or balliboe of Mullaghmehoagh in the territory of Munterevelinge Itragh, barony of Dungannon, County Tyrone, to William Cunningham for 3 years, dated 17 September 1659. [DP/Lenox-Conyngham pp]

STEWART, ANTHONY, mustered unarmed in the barony of Raphoe, County Donegal, 1630. [Donegal Muster Roll]

STEWART, ARCHIBALD, in Dublin, 1637. [NAS.GD406.1.359]

STEWART, ARCHIBALD, in Coleraine, 1642. [NAS.GD406.1.1307]

STEWART, ARCHIBALD, in the Routt or the Glens of Antrim, a witness in 1661. [CSP.Ire.1661]

STEWART, ARCHIBALD, leased lands in Ulster from the Marquis of Antrim on 21 January 1637. [CSPIre30.3.1666]

STEWART, CHARLES, with his wife Anna Hamilton, from County Tyrone, in Guthrie, Angus, in 1691. [NAS.CH2.535.1.303/63]

STEWART, JAMES, mustered unarmed in the barony of Raphoe, County Donegal, 1630. [Donegal Muster Roll]

STEWART, JAMES, a witness in Dungannon, County Tyrone, 8 March 1667. [CSPIre]

STEWART, JOHN, in Dungiven, County Londonderry, 1630. [Dungiven Muster Roll]

STEWART, JOHN, mustered with a sword in the barony of Raphoe, County Donegal, 1630. [Donegal Muster Roll]

STEWART, JOHN, mustered unarmed in the barony of Raphoe, County Donegal, 1630. [Donegal Muster Roll]

STEWART, JOHN, in the parish of Raphoe, County Donegal, 1665. [HTR]

STEWART, LUDOVICK, in the barony of Magherasterhana and Clankeilly, County Fermanagh, 1631. [Fermanagh Muster Roll]

STEWART, ROBERT, a witness in Dungannon, County Tyrone, 8 March 1667. [CSPIre]

STEWART, SAMUEL, Captain of Home of the Heugh's Regiment at Carrickfergus on 9 September 1642. [DS#336]

STEWART, W., an assizeman in Dungannon, County Tyrone, 8 March 1667. [CSPIre]

STEWART, WILLIAM, in barony of Raphoe, 1630. [Donegal Muster Roll]

STEWART, WILLIAM, a witness in Dungannon, County Tyrone, 8 March 1667. [CSPIre]

STIRLING, Sir ROBERT, a Colonel in the service of Kings Charles I and II, took refuge in Ireland around 1651, petitioned for lands in County Dublin and County Wicklow in 1663. [CSPIre]

STIRLING, THOMAS, in Dungiven, County Londonderry, 1630. [Dungiven Muster Roll]

STORY, DAVID, in the barony of Magherasterhana and Clankeilly, County Fermanagh, 1631. [Fermanagh Muster Roll]

STUART, HENRY, of Carrogen, 1646. [NAS.NRAS.104.2.34]

SWAYNE, JOHN, mustered with a sword and a pike in the barony of Raphoe, County Donegal, 1630. [Donegal Muster Roll]

TAYLOR, JOHN, mustered with unarmed in the barony of Raphoe, County Donegal, 1630. [Donegal Muster Roll]

TELFER, ROBERT, in the barony of Magherasterhana and Clankeilly, County Fermanagh, 1631. [Fermanagh Muster Roll]

THISTLE, LAWRENCE, a tenant of William Conyngham in Armagh, 1683. [DP]

THOMPSON, ALEXANDER, mustered unarmed in the barony of Raphoe, County Donegal, 1630. [Donegal Muster Roll]

THOMPSON, HUGH, mustered with sword and pike in the barony of Raphoe, County Donegal, 1630. [Donegal Muster Roll]

THOMPSON, JAMES, a carpenter in Dublin, 1723. [NAS.AC7.28.118-1139]

THOMPSON, JOHN, the elder, merchant in Coleraine, bond for 2000 merks with Hugh Thompson, flesher burgess of Irvine, 8 June 1688. [NAS.GD1.693.16]

THOMPSON, JOHN, of Sevenacres, merchant in Coleraine, only son and heir of the late John Thompson, merchant there, 11 August 1711. [NAS.GD1.693.19]

THOMPSON, JOHN, only son and heir of Hugh Thompson, merchant and sailor in Coleraine, County Antrim, and heir to his grandfather Hugh Thompson, flesher burgess of Irvine, 8 May 1728. [NAS.GD1.693.22]

THOMPSON, NINIAN, mustered with a sword and pike in the barony of Raphoe, County Donegal, 1630. [Donegal Muster Roll]

THOMPSON, THOMAS, in the parish of Raphoe, County Donegal, 1665. [HTR]

THOMSON, ARCHIBALD, in the country of Clannybowie, Ireland, 1630. [see Janet Archibald's testament, confirmed 23 March 1630, Glasgow. NAS.CC9]

THOMSON, GEORGE, burgess of Irvine, residing in Ireland, 1618. [AG.IV.15]

THOMSON, HUGH, a merchant burgess of Londonderry, 1615, 1619. [AG.VII.205; IV.105]

THOMSON, HUGH, mustered with sword and pike in the barony of Raphoe, County Donegal, 1630. [Donegal Muster Roll]

THOMSON, JOHN, in the barony of Magheraboy, County Fermanagh, 1631. [Fermanagh Muster Roll]

THOMSON, JOHN, tenant on William Cunningham's lands in County Londonderry, 1683. [DP/Lenox-Conyngham pp]

THOMSON, LEWIS, a merchant in Belfast, 1628. [NAS.AC7.1.196]

THOMSON, MATHEW, weaver and freeman of Newton, County Down, 1640. [HH.80]

THOMSON, WILLIAM, in the parish of Kilwaghter, 1652. [NAS.GD154.514]

THOMSON, WILLIAM, a witness, 5 August 1655. [NAS.RH15.91.38]

THORNTON, FRANCIS, master of the Russell Galley of Dublin, 1707. [NAS.AC9.243]

THURRAGOOD, CHARLES, master of the Harry of Dublin, from Leith to Dublin on 17 September 1667. [NAS.E72.15.6]

TIRROL, JOHN, in Stamuling, tanner in County Meath, 1714. [LI#403]

TORRANCE, JOHN, mustered unarmed in the barony of Raphoe, County Donegal, 1630. [Donegal Muster Roll]

TRAILL, JAMES, 1659. [NAS.RH15.91.38]

TRAILL, Mrs MARY, 13 November 1671. [NAS.RH15.91.40]

TRAN, ELIZABETH, spouse of Matthew Hommill a merchant in Irvine, Ayrshire, later in Dunluce, Ireland, 15 December 1618. [NAS.RS11.1.265]

TROTTER, FRANCIS, in the barony of Magheraboy, County Fermanagh, 1631. [Fermanagh Muster Roll]

TROTTER, GEORGE, in Dungiven, County Londonderry, 1630. [Dungiven Muster Roll]

TROTTER, THOMAS, in the barony of Magheraboy, County Fermanagh, 1631. [Fermanagh Muster Roll]

TRUMBLE, JOHN, mustered with a sword in the barony of Raphoe, County Donegal, 1630. [Donegal Muster Roll]

TRUMBLE, JOHN, in the barony of Magheraboy, County Fermanagh, 1631. [Fermanagh Muster Roll]

TRUMBLE, JOHN, in the parish of Kilwaghter, 1652. [NAS.GD154.514]

TULLAGH, DAVID, mustered unarmed in the barony of Raphoe, County Donegal, 1630. [Donegal Muster Roll]

TURNER, JAMES, Major of Lord Sinclair's Regiment in Newry on 28 September 1642. [DS#337]

TWEEDY, JANET, daughter of the late John Tweedie shipmaster burgess of Irvine, and wife of John Watson, schoolmaster of Bangour, 1620. [AG.IV.255]

VESEY, THOMAS, Bachelor in Divinity and minister of Coleraine, leased Machriboy More, Machriboy Begg, Bellimore Begg, in the parish of Killowen, County Londonderry, from John, Lord Kirkcudbright, on 11 December 1655. [NAS.RH15.91.32][PRONI.T640/80]

WALKER, ALEXANDER, in the parish of Raphoe, County Donegal, 1665. [HTR]

WALKER, CHRISTOPHER, mustered unarmed in the barony of Raphoe, County Donegal, 1630. [Donegal Muster Roll]

WALKER, DAVID, mustered with a sword and callener in the barony of Raphoe, County Donegal, 1630. [Donegal Muster Roll]

WALKER, JOHN, mustered with a sword in the barony of Raphoe, County Donegal, 1630. [Donegal Muster Roll]

WALKER, JOHN, of Findurk, in the parish of Raphoe, County Donegal, 1665. [HTR]

WALKER, JOHN, born 1667, a merchant from Belfast, emigrated via Liverpool to the Chesapeake on 6 October 1686. [LRO.QSP.625/2]

WALLACE, JAMES, Captain of Major General Robert Monro's Regiment in Carrickfergus on 9 September 1642. [DS#329]

WALLACE, JOHN, a workman in Ireland, 10 May 1621. [NAS.RS11.2.155]

WALLACE, JOHN, (1), mustered unarmed in the barony of Raphoe, County Donegal, 1630. [Donegal Muster Roll]

WALLACE, JOHN, (2), mustered unarmed in the barony of Raphoe, County Donegal, 1630. [Donegal Muster Roll]

WALLACE, JOHN, mustered with a snaphance in the barony of Raphoe, County Donegal, 1630. [Donegal Muster Roll]

WALLACE, MICHAEL, in the parish of Raphoe, County Donegal, 1665. [HTR]

WALLACE, ROBERT, mustered with a sword in the barony of Raphoe, Donegal, 1630. [Donegal Muster Roll]

WALLACE, ROBERT, of Roveagh, born 1665, died 11 November 1726. [Clogher Cathedral gravestone]

WALLACE, WILLIAM, mustered unarmed in the barony of Raphoe, County Donegal, 1630. [Donegal Muster Roll]

WALLACE, WILLIAM, witnessed a lease on 17 September 1659. [DP/Lenox-Conyngham pp]

WALTER, JOHN, in the parish of Raphoe, County Donegal, 1665. [HTR]

WALTER, WILLIAM, in the parish of Raphoe, County Donegal, 1665. [HTR]

WANN, WILLIAM, mustered with sword and snaphance in the barony of Raphoe, County Donegal, 1630. [Donegal Muster Roll]

WARK, JOHN, in Magiligan, County Londonderry, 9 August 1666. [NAS.RH15.91.40]

WATSON, GEORGE, mustered with a sword in the barony of Raphoe, County Donegal, 1630. [Donegal Muster Roll]

WATSON, JOHN, mustered unarmed in the barony of Raphoe, County Donegal, 1630. [Donegal Muster Roll]

WATSON, JOHN, schoolmaster in Bangour, husband of Janet Tweedie from Irvine, Ayrshire, 1620. [AG.IV.255]

WATSON, JOHN, mustered with sword and pike in the barony of Raphoe, County Donegal, 1630. [Donegal Muster Roll]

WATT, JOHN, mustered unarmed in the barony of Raphoe, County Donegal, 1630. [Donegal Muster Roll]

WATT, WILLIAM, a merchant in Dublin, 1666. [NAS.RH9.5.11, 31]

WATTERS, NINIAN, in Dungiven, County Londonderry, 1630. [Dungiven Muster Roll]

WATTERSON, JOHN, in the barony of Magheraboy, County Fermanagh, 1631. [Fermanagh Muster Roll]

WAUCHOPE, ROBERT, Captain of Major General Robert Monro's Regiment in Carrickfergus on 9 September 1642. [DS#329]

WAUSE, JOHN, mustered with a sword in the barony of Raphoe, County Donegal, 1630. [Donegal Muster Roll]

WHITE, ADAM, a non-conformist minister who had been imprisoned for seven years in Lifford gaol, petitioned King Charles II for his release, 1669. [CSPIre]

WHITE, ADAM, of Muthergill, town of Douglas, probably a Covenanting refugee, to Ireland by 1683. [RPCS.VIII.658]

WHITE, GEORGE, mustered with sword in the barony of Raphoe, County Donegal, 1630. [Donegal Muster Roll]

WHITE, ROBERT, mustered with a sword in the barony of Raphoe, County Donegal, 1630. [Donegal Muster Roll]

WHITE, ROBERT, mustered unarmed in the barony of Raphoe, County Donegal, 1630. [Donegal Muster Roll]

WHYTE, GILBERT, a yeoman in Killone parish, County Londonderry, leased Castle Tondery in the parish of Killone, on 8 August 1655. [PRONI.T640/71]

WIGHTON, WILLIAM, mustered unarmed in the barony of Raphoe, County Donegal, 1630. [Donegal Muster Roll]

WIGTON, ANDREW, in the parish of Raphoe, County Donegal, 1665. [HTR]

WIGTON, JOHN, in the parish of Raphoe, County Donegal, 1665. [HTR]

WILLIAMSON, Captain DAVID, provost of Killelagh, County Down, 1671, 1673. [NAS.RH15.91.38/40] [PRONI.T640/111/122]

WILLIAMSON, JAMES, 1672. [NAS.RH15.91.39]

WILSON, ALEXANDER, in the parish of Raphoe, County Donegal, 1665. [HTR]

WILSON, GEORGE, in Anlow, County Londonderry, 9 August 1666. [NAS.RH15.91.40]

WILSON, HUMPHREY, in the parish of Raphoe, County Donegal, 1665. [HTR]

WILSON, JAMES, mustered unarmed in the barony of Raphoe, County Donegal, 1630. [Donegal Muster Roll]

WILSON, JOHN, in barony of Raphoe, 1630. [Donegal Muster Roll]

WILSON, JOHN, mustered with a sword and pike in the barony of Raphoe, County Donegal, 1630. [Donegal Muster Roll]

WILSON, JOHN, a seaman from Ardrossan, Ayrshire, who settled in Ireland by 1684. [RPCS.IX.553]

WILSON, MICHAEL, in the barony of Magherstefeny (?), County Fermanagh, 1631. [Fermanagh Muster Roll]

WILSON, RICHARD, in the parish of Raphoe, County Donegal, 1665. [HTR]

WILSON, ROBERT, mustered with a sword in the barony of Raphoe, County Donegal, 1630. [Donegal Muster Roll]

WILSON, ROBERT, in the barony of Magheraboy, County Fermanagh, 1631. [Fermanagh Muster Roll]

WILSON, ROBERT, witnessed a lease on 17 September 1659. [DP/Lenox-Conyngham pp]

WILSON, ROBERT, a merchant in Belfast, 1722. [NAS.AC9.849]

WILSON, WILLIAM, mustered with sword and pike in the barony of Raphoe, County Donegal, 1630. [Donegal Muster Roll]

WILSON, WILLIAM, master of the Donegal of Belfast, from Ireland to Catalonia in December 1705. [Cal.SPDom.42/119/193]

WOOD, ANDREW, mustered with a sword in the barony of Raphoe, County Donegal, 1630. [Donegal Muster Roll]

WOOD, JAMES, mustered with a sword in the barony of Raphoe, County Donegal, 1630. [Donegal Muster Roll]

WOOD, JOHN, mustered unarmed in the barony of Raphoe, County Donegal, 1630. [Donegal Muster Roll]

WOOD, JOHN, mustered with a sword in the barony of Raphoe, Donegal, 1630. [Donegal Muster Roll]

WOOD, RICHARD, in Bellimacarran, 7 September 1675. [PRONI.T640/127]

WOOD, WILLIAM, mustered unarmed in the barony of Raphoe, County Donegal, 1630. [Donegal Muster Roll]

WRIGHT, PATRICK, mustered unarmed in the barony of Raphoe, County Donegal, 1630. [Donegal Muster Roll]

WRIGHT, PATRICK, reference on 24 December 1672. [NAS.RH15.91.39]

WRIGHT, SAMUEL, a gentleman, a petition dated 11 October 1638. [PRONI.T640/42]

WRIGHT, WILLIAM, in the parish of Raphoe, County Donegal, 1665. [HTR]

WYLIE, WILLIAM, in Dungiven, County Londonderry, 1630. [Dungiven Muster Roll]

WYLLIE, CATHARINE, only daughter of Robert Wyllie in Carnecassill, County Antrim, spouse of Thomas Reid in Mayokill, County Londonderry, heir to her uncle Hugh Wyllie, son of the late John Wyllie at the mill of Ardrossan, Ayrshire, 5 February 1661. [NAS.GD1/693/6]

WYLLIE, JOHN, mustered with a sword and pike in the barony of Raphoe, County Donegal, 1630. [Donegal Muster Roll]

WYLLIE, JOHN, mustered with a sword and snaphance in the barony of Raphoe, County Donegal, 1630. [Donegal Muster Roll]

WYLLIE, JOHN, mustered with a snaphance in the barony of Raphoe, County Donegal, 1630. [Donegal Muster Roll]

WYLLIE, MUNGO, mustered with sword and pike in the barony of Raphoe, County Donegal, 1630. [Donegal Muster Roll]

WYLLIE, THOMAS, of Cessnecully, in the parish of Raphoe, County Donegal, 1665. [HTR]

YOUNG, DAVID, mustered unarmed in the barony of Raphoe, County Donegal, 1630. [Donegal Muster Roll]

YOUNG, JAMES, mustered with a sword and snaphance in the barony of Raphoe, Donegal, 1630. [Donegal Muster Roll]

YOUNG, JOHN, mustered unarmed in the barony of Raphoe, County Donegal, 1630. [Donegal Muster Roll]

YOUNG, JOHN, in Coreane, leased Bellymor in the parish of Dunboe, County Londonderry, on 10 November 1655. [PRONI.T640/81]

YOUNG, ROBERT, mustered with a sword in the barony of Raphoe, Donegal, 1630. [Donegal Muster Roll]

YOUNG, WILLIAM, in Dungiven, County Londonderry, 1630. [Dungiven Muster Roll]

YOUNG, WILLIAM, (1), mustered unarmed in the barony of Raphoe, County Donegal, 1630. [Donegal Muster Roll]

YOUNG, WILLIAM, (2), mustered unarmed in the barony of Raphoe, County Donegal, 1630. [Donegal Muster Roll]

YULE, ALEXANDER, schoolmaster at Stirling Grammar School, was given leave of absence to go to Ireland and settle his servants on the lands that the had leased from Adam Abercrombie, 25 September 1607. [SBR]